THE CALIFORNIA DIRECTORY OF
FINE WINERIES

SECOND EDITION

THE CALIFORNIA DIRECTORY OF

FineWineries

MARTY OLMSTEAD, WRITER

ROBERT HOLMES, PHOTOGRAPHER

TOM SILBERKLEIT, EDITOR AND PUBLISHER

WINE HOUSE PRESS

CONTENTS

INTRODUCTION

Whether you are a visitor or a native seeking the ultimate chalice of nectar from the grape, navigating Northern California's wine country can be intimidating. Hundreds of wineries—from glamorous estates to converted barns, from nationally recognized labels to hidden gems—are found throughout Napa, Sonoma, and Mendocino. The challenge is deciding where to go and how to plan a trip. This book will be your indispensable traveling companion.

The sixty wineries in this fully updated, second edition of *The California Directory of Fine Wineries* are known for producing some of the world's most admired wines. From the moment you walk in the door of these wineries, you will be greeted like a guest and invited to sample at a relaxing, leisurely tempo. Although the quality of the winemaker's art is of paramount importance, the wineries are also notable as tourist destinations. Many boast award-winning contemporary architecture, while others are housed in lovingly preserved historical structures. Some have galleries featuring museum-quality artwork by local and international artists or exhibits focusing on the region's past and the history of winemaking. You will also enjoy taking informative behind-the-scenes tours, exploring inspirational gardens, and participating in celebrated culinary programs.

As you explore this magnificent region, you'll encounter some of California's most appealing scenery and attractions—mountain ranges, rugged coastline, pastures with majestic oak trees, abundant parkland, renowned spas, and historic towns. Use the information in this book to plan your trip, and be sure to stop along the way and take in the sights. You have my promise that traveling to your destination will be as sweet as the wine tasted upon your welcome.

—Tom Silberkleit
Editor and Publisher
Wine House Press
Sonoma, California

THE ETIQUETTE OF WINE TASTING

While most of the wineries profiled in this book offer amenities ranging from lush gardens to art exhibitions, their main attraction is the tasting room. This is where winery employees get a chance to share their products and knowledge with consumers, in hopes of establishing a lifelong relationship. They are there to please.

Yet, for some visitors, the ritual of tasting fine wines can be intimidating. Perhaps it's because swirling wine and using a spit bucket seem to be unnatural acts. But with a few tips, even a first-time taster can enjoy the experience. After all, the point of tasting is to enhance your knowledge by learning the differences among varieties of wines, styles of winemaking, and appellations.

A list of available wines is posted in most tasting rooms, beginning with whites and ending with the heaviest reds. You can ask the pourer for suggestions or simply request wines that interest you. After you are served the wine, hold the stem of the glass with your thumb and as many fingers as you need to maintain control. Lift the glass up to the light and note the color and intensity. Good wines tend to be bright, with the color fading near the rim.

Next, gently swirl the wine in the glass to aerate it, releasing additional aromas. Observe how much of the wine adheres to the sides of the glass. If lines—called legs—are visible, the wine is viscous, indicating body or weight as well as a high alcohol content. Now, tip the glass to about a 45-degree angle, take a short sniff, and concentrate on the aromas. Take another sniff and see if it reminds you of anything—rose petals, a freshly ironed pillowcase, or honey, for example—that will help you identify the aroma.

Finally, take a sip and swirl the wine around your tongue, letting your taste buds pick up all the flavors. It may taste of toast or cherries or mint—as with the "nosing," try to make as many associations as you can. Then spit the wine into the bucket. Afterward, notice how long the flavor stays in your mouth; a long finish is the ideal. If you don't want another taste, just pour the wine into the bucket and move on. Remember, the more you spit or pour out, the more wines you can taste. Many tasting rooms offer flavorless crackers for freshening your palate between wines.

The next level of wine tasting involves guided tastings and food-and-wine pairings. Often a few cheeses or a series of appetizers will be paired with a flight of wines, usually a selection of three red or three white wines presented in the correct order of tasting. The server will make it clear what goes with what.

If you still feel self-conscious, you can practice at home by swirling water in a glass, taking a sniff and a sip, and spitting it out into a bucket. When you return to the tasting room, you'll be more comfortable focusing on the wine itself—that's the real payoff, because once you learn what you like and why you like it, you'll be able to recognize wines in a similar vein anywhere in the world.

What Is an Appellation?

People who make, market, or consume fine wines often use the word *appellation* to refer to the geographical area where the grapes were grown. Inclusion of the appellation on the bottle label means that 85 percent of the wine is from that area.

The terms "appellation of origin" and "American Viticultural Area" (AVA) are frequently used interchangeably in casual conversation, but they are not synonymous. In the United States, appellations follow geopolitical borders, such as state and county lines, rather than geographic boundaries. AVAs are defined by such natural features as soil types, climate, and topography.

Since 1978, the U.S. Bureau of Alcohol, Tobacco and Firearms has been the arbiter of what does and does not qualify as an AVA. If a winery or group of wineries wants a particular area to qualify as an official AVA, they must prove that it has specific attributes that distinguish it significantly from its neighbors.

Why do winemakers care about this distinction? It is far more prestigious—and informative—to belong to an appellation such as Sonoma Valley, Napa Valley, or Russian River Valley than the more generic California, which means the grapes could have come from the Central Valley or anywhere else in the state. Informed consumers learn that a Chardonnay from the Alexander Valley, for instance, is apt to taste different from one originating in the Russian River Valley.

It's worth noting that a winery may be located in one appellation but use grapes from another to make a particular wine. In that case, the appellation used would be that of the source. For example, Ledson Winery and Vineyards is in the Sonoma Valley but makes a Pinot Noir using grapes from the Russian River Valley. Thus the bottle is labeled "Ledson Winery and Vineyards Pinot Noir, Russian River Valley."

The following are the appellations in Napa, Sonoma, and Mendocino:

NAPA	SONOMA	MENDOCINO
Atlas Peak	Alexander Valley	Anderson Valley
Carneros	Bennett Valley	Cole Ranch
Chiles Valley District	Carneros	Hopland Valley
Diamond Mountain District	Chalk Hill	McDowell Valley
Howell Mountain	Dry Creek Valley	Mendocino
Mount Veeder	Green Valley	Mendocino Ridge
Napa Valley	Knight's Valley	Potter Valley
Oak Knoll District	Northern Sonoma	Redwood Valley
Oakville	Rockpile	Ukiah Valley
Rutherford	Russian River Valley	(proposed viticultural area)
Spring Mountain District	Sonoma Coast	Yorkville Highlands
St. Helena	Sonoma Mountain	
Stags Leap District	Sonoma Valley	
Wild Horse Valley		
Yountville		

NAPA

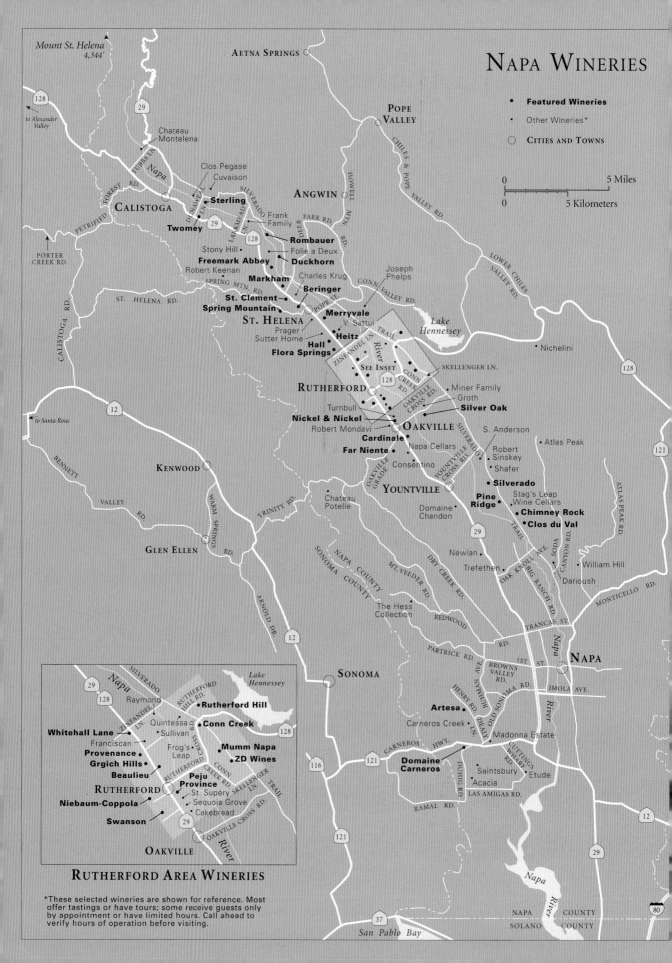

Napa Wineries

- Featured Wineries
- Other Wineries*
- Cities and Towns

Rutherford Area Wineries

*These selected wineries are shown for reference. Most offer tastings or have tours; some receive guests only by appointment or have limited hours. Call ahead to verify hours of operation before visiting.

The most famous winemaking region in the United States, the Napa Valley is a microcosm of the wine country, with hundreds of wineries and thousands of acres of vineyards amassed in a narrow valley less than thirty miles long. This patchwork of agriculture extends north from upper San Pablo Bay to the dramatic palisades beside Calistoga. On the east, it is defined by a series of hills known as the Vaca Range. The western horizon is dominated by the rugged peaks of the Mayacamas Range, including the steep inclines and forested slopes of Mount Veeder.

The best way to get an overview is to take a hot-air balloon ride that departs at daybreak for a cool, calm flight above the vineyards and usually concludes with a champagne breakfast. The second-best way is to drive up the Oakville Grade and pull over at the top for a postcard-perfect view.

The county's largest cities are Napa and St. Helena, where you will find many shops and major attractions. Charming small towns along Highway 29, the main thoroughfare that is mostly only two lanes wide, have restaurants, inns, spas, and other businesses that cater to visitors.

ARTESA VINEYARDS AND WINERY

Virtually the entire Carneros appellation is visible from this property, built into a hilltop in the southern Napa Valley. Despite this wraparound view, the winery itself is a more compelling vision. As visitors approach it, the entrance is hidden from sight. At the base of the staircase leading to Artesa, six abstract sculptures by artist-in-residence Gordon Huether encircle the main fountain. Only after mounting the steep double stairway to the plaza can visitors see the entry doors, dug into a hillside covered with native grasses. On this level are more fountains, spewing arches of water that collapse into tranquil pools. With its tiered construction, the winery is reminiscent of a hidden Mayan temple.

The modernist winery was designed by renowned Barcelona architect Domingo Triay and executed by Napa Valley architect Earl R. Bouligny. The 120,000-square-foot structure was created by removing 30 feet of hilltop and then matching the facility's height to the original elevation. As a result, the building is naturally insulated.

The winery began life as Codorniu Napa, which produced sparkling wines exclusively. In 1999, eight years after the $30 million facility opened, it was rechristened Artesa, which means "craftsman" in the Spanish Catalan language of the owners, the Raventos family. The Raventos also own Codorniu in Catalonia, where the family boasts 450 years of winemaking experience and a 125-year history as one of Europe's leading producers of sparkling wine made in the traditional *méthode champenoise*. Rather than fermented in a barrel, the wine is fermented in the bottle from which it will be poured. The transformation into a facility that also specializes in still wines took three years and $10 million.

The winery interior has a peaceful courtyard with sculptures, a fountain, and a pool of water. The tasting room with its curved wooden bar has a picture-window view of the courtyard. Artesa's commitment to fine arts is revealed in its extensive collection, including a large bronze by Spanish sculptor Marcel Marti in front of a reflecting pool. Gordon Huether exhibits works in various media, particularly glass and metal, throughout the visitor center. Among the newer features are a museum and the Carneros Center, which educates visitors about the human history, natural history, topography, and scenic beauty of the appellation. The museum displays antique winemaking equipment, including sixteenth-century Spanish wine casks and Greek wine cups from 400 B.C.

Looking closely at the Artesa label, one sees elements of the winery's architecture, its sculpture, and its prismlike windows, as well as a triangle, a shape representing balance that is repeated often throughout the property. The label's use of gold signifies, of course, excellence.

ARTESA VINEYARDS AND WINERY
1345 Henry Rd.
Napa, CA 94559
707-224-1668
info@artesawinery.com
www.artesawinery.com

OWNER: Codorniu.

LOCATION: About 7 miles southwest of the town of Napa.

APPELLATION: Carneros.

HOURS: 10 A.M.–5 P.M. daily.

TASTINGS: $6 for 6 wines; $10 for 5 reserve wines.

TOURS: 11 A.M. and 2 P.M.; self-guided tours during operating hours.

THE WINES: Cabernet Sauvignon, Chardonnay, late-harvest Gewürztraminer, Merlot, Pinot Noir, Sauvignon Blanc, sparkling wines, Syrah.

SPECIALTIES: Multiple bottlings of major varietals by appellation.

WINEMAKER: Don Van Staaveren.

ANNUAL PRODUCTION: 80,000 cases.

OF SPECIAL NOTE: Sparkling wine available only at winery; some limits on reserve wines. Art exhibitions and museum displays on local and European winemaking.

NEARBY ATTRACTIONS: di Rosa Preserve (indoor and outdoor exhibits of works by contemporary Bay Area artists).

15

BEAULIEU VINEYARD

BEAULIEU VINEYARD
1960 Hwy. 29
Rutherford, CA 94573
707-967-5233
www.bvwines.com

OWNER: Diageo Chateau
& Estates Wines.

LOCATION: About 3 miles
south of St. Helena.

APPELLATION: Napa Valley.

HOURS: 10 A.M.–5 P.M. daily.

TASTINGS: $5 for 4 or 5 wines
in Main Tasting Room;
$25 for 5 reserve wines in
Georges De Latour Reserve
Room.

TOURS: Call 707-967-5233
for information.

THE WINES: Cabernet
Sauvignon, Chardonnay,
Merlot, Muscat, Pinot Gris,
Pinot Noir, Port, Sangiovese,
Sauvignon Blanc, Syrah,
Viognier, Zinfandel

SPECIALTY: Georges De
Latour Private Reserve
Cabernet Sauvignon.

WINEMAKERS: Joel Aiken,
Robert Masyzcek, and
Jeffrey Stambor.

ANNUAL PRODUCTION:
1.5 million cases.

OF SPECIAL NOTE: Tastings
of Signet Series, a line of
limited production wines,
on first weekend of each
month ($5). Various special
tastings and events, and
educational programs; call
for details.

NEARBY ATTRACTIONS:
Bothe-Napa State Park
(hiking, picnicking, horse-
back riding, swimming
Memorial Day–Labor Day);
Bale Grist Mill State Historic
Park (water-powered mill
circa 1846); Culinary
Institute of America at
Greystone (cooking
demonstrations); Silverado
Museum (Robert Louis
Stevenson memorabilia).

The roots of Beaulieu Vineyard were firmly planted in Napa Valley by Frenchman Georges De Latour, a native of Bordeaux, in 1900, when he established a winery on the 4 acres where he lived in Rutherford. He named it Beaulieu, meaning "beautiful place." Within a few years, he purchased 128 acres of prime vineyard land adjacent to his home, then later bought more land near Oakville. Today, these vineyards, which are still called BV#1 and BV#2, are at the heart of Beaulieu Vineyard's production of Private Reserve and Rutherford Cabernet Sauvignon.

De Latour was highly visionary in his approach to the business of winemaking. He developed a relationship with the Catholic Church to provide altar wine, thereby allowing Beaulieu to stay in operation legally during Prohibition. His genius was proven again in 1938, when he hired a young Russo-French enologist, André Tchelistcheff. Tchelistcheff's influence was immediate and dramatic: he put Beaulieu on the map by producing a series of award-winning Cabernets, as well as by developing techniques and technologies used by many of today's winemakers, including Joel Aiken, the current vice president of winemaking.

Tchelistcheff had a remarkable ability to teach and inspire young winemakers, and his insights and knowledge touched three generations of winemakers in Napa Valley and beyond. Tchelistcheff had an in-depth understanding of fermentation science, including temperature-controlled fermentation processes that enhance the balance of fine wines. Under Tchelistcheff's guidance, Beaulieu created wines in the tradition and style of the great chateaus of France.

With its ivy-clad stone buildings and red-tile roofs, Beaulieu Vineyard is one of the prettiest wineries in Napa. Looking at the historic structures, visitors can imagine the time when Beaulieu's winery was essentially the only building along a stretch of unpaved road that is now Highway 29. The winery's older structures are the work of Hamdon McIntire, who also designed Inglenook, Greystone, and Far Niente.

Adjacent to the winemaking facilities is a small, wisteria-shaded building where visitors can sample Georges De Latour Private Reserve Cabernet Sauvignon, Tapestry Reserve, and the new Dulcet Reserve wines. The Private Reserve Cabernet Sauvignon was California's first prestige bottling. No California winery can offer a bottled record to match the sixty-five vintages of Private Reserve stretching from 1936 to 2001 (with the exception of 1937). The Main Tasting Room lies beyond, in an octagonal structure that offers BV's Appellation and Signet wines, including Rutherford Cabernet. A tasteful gift shop beckons at the bottom of a spiral staircase.

BERINGER VINEYARDS

With the 1883 Rhine House, hand-carved aging tunnels, and a heritage dating to 1876, Beringer Vineyards is steeped in history like few other wineries in California. The oldest continuously operating winery in the Napa Valley, it combines age-old traditions with up-to-date technology to create a wide range of award-winning wines.

It was German know-how that set the Beringer brothers on the path to glory. Jacob and Frederick Beringer emigrated from Mainz, Germany, to the United States in the 1860s. Jacob, having worked in cellars in Germany, was intrigued when he heard that the California climate was ideal for growing the varietal grapes that flourished in Europe's winemaking regions. Leaving Frederick in New York, he traveled west in 1870 to discover that the Napa Valley's rocky, well-drained soils were similar to those in his native Rhine Valley. Five years later, he bought land with Frederick and began excavating the hillsides to create tunnels for aging his wines. The brothers founded Beringer Vineyards in 1876. During the building of the caves and winery, Jacob lived in

an 1848 farmhouse now known as the Hudson House. The meticulously restored and expanded structure now serves as Beringer Vineyards' Culinary Arts Center.

But the star attraction on the lavishly landscaped grounds is unquestionably the seventeen-room Rhine House, which Frederick modeled after his ancestral home in Germany. The redwood, brick, and stucco mansion is painted in the original Tudor color scheme of earth tones, and the original slate still covers the gabled roof and exterior. The interior is graced with myriad gems of craftsmanship such as Belgian art nouveau–style stained-glass windows.

The winery's standard tour encompasses a visit to the cellars and the hand-dug aging tunnels in the Old Stone Winery, where tasting is available. Beringer also offers programs that provide visitors more in-depth experiences. The Vintage Legacy Tour focuses on the winery's history. The Historic District Tour emphasizes points of historic interest such as the Rhine House and aging caves. The Picnic at Beringer Tour starts at the original St. Helena Home Vineyard and proceeds through the Old Stone Winery prior to a three-course alfresco lunch in the Redwood Grove, prepared by Beringer Vineyards executive chef David Frakes.

BERINGER VINEYARDS
2000 Main St.
St. Helena, CA 94574
707-963-4812
www.beringer.com

OWNER: Beringer Blass Wine Estates.

LOCATION: On Hwy. 29 about .5 mile north of St. Helena.

APPELLATION: Napa Valley.

HOURS: 10 A.M.–5 P.M. daily in winter; 10 A.M.–6 P.M. daily in summer.

TASTINGS: 2 wines with tour fee; $5 for 3 nonreserve wines in Old Stone Winery; $10–20 for reserve wine flights.

TOURS: 30-minute tours ($5) on the hour, 10 A.M.– 4 P.M. Vintage Legacy Tour ($30), Historic District Tour ($18), and Picnic at Beringer ($65) by reservation.

THE WINES: Cabernet Franc, Cabernet Sauvignon, Cabernet Sauvignon Port, Chardonnay, Johannisberg Riesling, Merlot, Petite Sirah, Pinot Grigio, Pinot Noir, Sangiovese, Sauvignon Blanc, Sparkling White Zinfandel, Syrah, White Merlot, White Zinfandel.

SPECIALTIES: Private Reserve Cabernet Sauvignon, Single-Vineyard Cabernet Sauvignon, Private Reserve Chardonnay.

WINEMAKERS:
Ed Sbragia, wine master; Laurie Hook, winemaker.

ANNUAL PRODUCTION:
Unavailable.

OF SPECIAL NOTE: Tour includes visit to barrel storage caves hand-chiseled by Chinese laborers in late 1800s.

NEARBY ATTRACTIONS:
Bothe-Napa State Park (hiking, picnicking, horseback riding, swimming Memorial Day–Labor Day); Bale Grist Mill State Historic Park (water-powered mill circa 1846); Silverado Museum (Robert Louis Stevenson memorabilia).

CARDINALE ESTATE

CARDINALE ESTATE
7600 Hwy. 29
Oakville, CA 94562
707-948-2643
info@cardinale.com
www.cardinale.com

OWNERS: Jackson family.

LOCATION: East side of Hwy. 29 just north of Yountville.

APPELLATION: Oakville.

HOURS: 10:30 A.M.–4 P.M. daily.

TASTINGS: $10–$25 for counter tastings; $30 for sit-down tastings by appointment.

TOURS: None.

THE WINES: Cardinale (Bordeaux blend).

SPECIALTIES: Cardinale (Bordeaux blend).

WINEMAKERS: Chris Carpenter (Lokoya and Cardinale labels) and Tom Peffer (Atalon).

ANNUAL PRODUCTION: 13,000 cases.

OF SPECIAL NOTE: Lokoya (Cabernet Sauvignon from specific appellations in Napa Valley) and Atalon (Napa Valley Cabernet Sauvignon and Merlot) wines are also available for tasting.

NEARBY ATTRACTIONS: Napa Valley Museum (winemaking displays, art exhibits).

Situated in the renowned Oakville District, Cardinale Estate winery is perched atop a knoll that commands a panoramic view of the Napa Valley. On the southwest side of the winery, a balcony affords visitors the unique opportunity to view the lay of the land and locate the world-famous appellations along the valley floor, as well as along the Mayacamas and Vaca ranges. For those who want to study a particular location in detail, a telescope is available.

Surrounding the winery are low fieldstone walls built more than a century ago. Below to the east are fields and vineyards and an old farmhouse that has been standing there since the late nineteenth century. Inside the winery, however, is a twenty-first-century operation that produces an ultra- premium Bordeaux blend that influ- ential critic Robert Parker deemed "one of the profound wines being produced in northern California."

Cardinale's contemporary Italian architecture befits its lofty location. On the east side of the building, four square stone pillars, entwined with climbing roses, support a pergola above a flooring of decomposed gran- ite. On the west side, a little courtyard is closed in by a stone wall covered with vines curling above pink coral bells and other plants. The Mediter- ranean theme continues inside the tasting room, with its travertine marble floor and stone-topped bar. The design of the interior is under- stated: cream-colored walls, maple furnishings, and a simple ivory chandelier. The minimalist decor balances the experience of sampling the wine or appreciating the spectacular scenery visible from the tasting room. Visitors can also enjoy the wine outside, at glass-topped tables on a marble-floored deck, where they have views of Mount Howell and one of Cardinale's mountain estate vineyards.

The profundity that Robert Parker wrote about derives from the mountain terrain of the core vineyards. Cardinale wine is primarily crafted from fruit grown on two rugged mountain estate vineyards—Keyes Vineyard on Howell Mountain and Veeder Peak Vineyard on Mount Veeder. The steep slopes have thin, rocky soils that force the vines to struggle, resulting in small berries that produce more concentrated flavors and colors than grapes grown on the valley floor with its richer soils. The rocks in the mountain soils also provide excellent drainage as well as trace elements that contribute to the complexity of the wines. Moreover, because of inversion—cold air settles on the valley floor while warm air rises—the higher elevations enjoy a longer growing season. Cardinale's special mountain vineyards have contributed to the wine's distinctive fusion of power and elegance since the 1995 vintage.

Chimney Rock Winery

Shaded by a grove of poplar trees, Chimney Rock's pristine white Cape Dutch buildings, with their steep, slate-gray roofs and curving, arched gables, complement their pastoral setting. The distinctive architecture was inspired by the many years that the winery's founders spent in South Africa. The late Sheldon "Hack" Wilson and his wife, Stella, had worked abroad for decades in the soft drink, brewing, restaurant, and luxury hotel businesses, developing a taste for fine wine along the way. Not surprisingly, they began their search for winery property in France. When a couple of potential sites in Bordeaux failed to materialize, they turned their attention to California and found what they were looking for in the Napa Valley.

Wilson's research convinced him that the soils and microclimates of the Stags Leap District would produce the quality of grapes for the style of wine he had in mind. When he saw the rustic Chimney Rock Golf Course, he could easily envision rows of grapevines in place of fairways. In 1980, the Wilsons purchased the golf course as well as the adjacent mountain, bulldozed nine of the eighteen holes, and planted vineyards on seventy-five acres. The first vintage was produced in 1984, and the winery's production building was completed five years later.

Douglas Fletcher was already an old hand at Stags Leap winemaking when he came on board in 1987, having worked at nearby Steltzner Vineyards. He was joined by assistant winemaker Elizabeth Vianna, a Brazilian-born enologist who had worked at Chimney Rock as an intern in 1999. Together, they focus on handcrafting wines mostly from Bordeaux varietals.

In 2000, the remaining fairways at Chimney Rock were converted to sixty-three acres of Cabernet Sauvignon vineyards. All of the winery's red-wine vineyards are in the Stags Leap District. The colorful name of this part of southern Napa stems from the legend of an agile buck seen bounding along a jagged outcropping of rock to elude hunters. The appellation extends south along the Silverado Trail from the Yountville Cross Road for three miles, bordered on the east by craggy hillsides and on the west by the Napa River.

Picturesque at any time of year, Chimney Rock Winery is especially appealing in spring and summer, when aromatic mauve Angel Face roses climb the columns in front of the hospitality center. The tasting room has white walls and dark exposed beams. On the far side, doors open onto a courtyard set with tables, chairs, and white market umbrellas and planted with a bevy of rosebushes bearing ivory flowers.

Chimney Rock Winery
5350 Silverado Trail
Napa, CA 94558
707-257-2641
www.chimneyrock.com

Owners: Terlato Wine Group and Wilson family.

Location: 3 miles south of Yountville.

Appellation: Stags Leap District.

Hours: 10 A.M.–5 P.M. daily.

Tastings: $7 for 4 wines.

Tours: Group tours by appointment.

The Wines: Cabernet Franc, Cabernet Sauvignon, Elevage (red Meritage).

Specialty: Cabernet Sauvignon.

Winemaker: Douglas Fletcher.

Annual Production: 18,000 cases.

Of Special Note: Some limited-production wines available only in tasting room.

Nearby Attractions: Napa Valley Opera House (live performances in historic building); Napa Valley Museum (winemaking displays, art exhibits).

CLOS DU VAL

CLOS DU VAL
5330 Silverado Trail
Napa, CA 94558
707-259-2200
800-993-9463
cdv@closduval.com
www.closduval.com

OWNER: John Goelet.

LOCATION: 5 miles north of the town of Napa.

APPELLATION: Napa Valley.

HOURS: 10 A.M.–5 P.M. daily.

TASTINGS: $5 for 4 wines (applicable to wine purchase).

TOURS: By appointment.

THE WINES: Cabernet Sauvignon, Chardonnay, Merlot, Pinot Noir.

SPECIALTY: Cabernet Sauvignon.

WINEMAKERS: Bernard Portet, John Clews, and Kian Tavakoli.

ANNUAL PRODUCTION: 65,000–70,000 cases.

OF SPECIAL NOTE: Library wines available for purchase. Reserve wines available only in the tasting room. *Pétanque* court and picnic area in olive grove.

NEARBY ATTRACTIONS: COPIA: The American Center for Wine, Food and the Arts; Napa Valley Museum (winemaking displays, art exhibits); Napa Valley Opera House (live performances in historic building).

That this winery has a French name is not an affectation. Owner and cofounder John Goelet's mother was a direct descendant of Françoise Guestier, a native of Bordeaux who worked for the Marquis de Segur, owner of Chateau Lafite and Latour. Clos Du Val translates as "small vineyard estate of a small valley," a modest nomenclature for a winery of its stature.

When Goelet, who is also the son of an American entrepreneur, set out on a global search for premium vineyard land, he found the ideal partner in Bernard Portet. Born in Cognac and raised in Bordeaux, Portet is a descendant of six generations of winemakers. He followed his passion with formal studies at the French winemaking schools of Toulouse and Montpelier before Goelet hired him in 1970 to establish Clos Du Val.

Portet spent two years searching five continents before getting a taste of the Napa Valley climate—or, technically, its  microclimates. At the time, the cool evenings and dramatic terrain of the Stags Leap District were relatively undiscovered by winemakers. Goelet proved his faith in Portet by promptly acquiring 150 acres of land in the district. The first vintage of the new venture was a 1972 Cabernet Sauvignon, one of only five California Cabernets selected for the now-legendary "Paris Tasting" in 1976, an event that put the world on notice that the Napa Valley was a winemaking force to watch. Ten years later, the same vintage took first place in a rematch, further enhancing Clos Du Val's reputation for creating wines that stand the test of time.

In 1973, Clos Du Val purchased 180 acres in another little-recognized appellation—Carneros in southern Napa. Thirteen years later, the winery released its first Carneros Chardonnay, and four years later, its first Carneros Pinot Noir.

A driveway lined with cypress trees leads to the imposing, vine-covered stone winery, behind which the dramatic rock outcroppings of Stags Leap rise in sharp relief. In front of the tasting room are Mediterranean-style gardens, a raised lawn area with tables and chairs defined by a hedge of boxwood, and a demonstration vineyard with twenty rows of Merlot grapevines, accompanied by brief explanations of vineyard management techniques. Inside the winery, halogen lights on the high ceiling beam down on the wooden tasting bar, the unglazed earth-toned tile floor, and a corner display of merchandise bearing the winery's distinctive, curlicued logo. Glass doors on the far side look into a large fermentation room filled with oak and steel tanks. Visitors are welcome to prolong their visit by playing pétanque or enjoying a picnic in the olive grove.

CONN CREEK WINERY

Conn Creek is one of the easiest-to-find wineries in the Napa Valley. Located near a well-traveled Rutherford intersection, it is housed in a simple Spanish Mediterranean-style stucco building that blends in well with the surroundings. In front, a grove of olive trees and colorful perennials thrive year-round in the California sun.

The winery was founded by William Collins, a former submarine officer, and his wife, Kathy, who named it for a seasonal tributary of the Napa River that flows through their vineyards. They planted grapes in 1967 and, six years later, established the winery and produced their first vintage. Conn Creek quickly won recognition for its red wines, particularly the 1974 Eisele Vineyard Cabernet Sauvignon. Most of the grapes for the award-winning wines produced in the early years came from the Collins Vineyard, which is so rocky that the owners had to use dynamite to break up the soil before planting. Situated alongside Highway 29 in St. Helena, Collins Vineyard has fifty-four acres of Cabernet Sauvignon, Cabernet Franc, and Merlot. Although Collins sold his winery in 1986, he maintains an exclusive long-term grape contract with Conn Creek.

The new owners, Ste. Michelle Wine Estates, decided to devote their energies to producing world-class red wines, paring Chardonnay and Zinfandel from the winery's product line to do so. The legendary André Tchelistcheff, the former winemaker at Beaulieu Vineyards and a longtime consultant to Ste. Michelle, participated in the winery's transition to limited-production Bordeaux varietals. By 1990, the winery had been retooled for its new focus, with an expanded barrel room, improved storage, and the acquisition of new French oak barrels.

More changes were to come. In 1994, Conn Creek's sister winery, the higher-production Villa Mt. Eden, moved into the winery, which was then renamed Villa Mt. Eden but continued to produce Conn Creek wines as well. While Villa Mt. Eden wines continue to be sold at the winery, in early 2003, the St. Helena winery was rededicated as the Conn Creek Winery and opened with a refurbished facility, retail shop, and barrel room. It also had a new winemaker, Jeff McBride, who had been winemaker at both Kenwood Vineyards and Dry Creek Vineyard in Sonoma County.

Throughout all these transitions, Conn Creek continued to pursue the goal of remaining a limited-production facility specializing in Bordeaux-style reds. To meet demand for its wines, the winery sources most of its grapes from the four-acre estate and the Collins vineyards, as well as from Palisades Ranch in the north valley (Cabernet Sauvignon) and Stagecoach Vineyard in Napa's rugged eastern hills, a prized growing area for Cabernet Franc and Merlot.

CONN CREEK WINERY
8711 Silverado Trail
St. Helena, CA 94574
707-963-9100
info@conncreek.com
www.conncreek.com

OWNER: Ste. Michelle Wine Estates.

LOCATION: Intersection of Silverado Trail and Rutherford Cross Rd.

APPELLATION: Napa Valley.

HOURS: 10 A.M.– 4 P.M. daily.

TASTINGS: $5 for 4 wines.

TOURS: By appointment, 10 A.M.–3 P.M.

THE WINES: Anthology (red Bordeaux-style blend), Cabernet Franc, Cabernet Sauvignon, Merlot, Sauvignon Blanc.

SPECIALTIES: Bordeaux varietals, especially Cabernet Sauvignon.

WINEMAKER: Jeff McBride.

ANNUAL PRODUCTION: 15,000 cases.

OF SPECIAL NOTE: Barrel sampling and blending seminars by appointment. Conn Creek Sauvignon Blanc available only at tasting room, which also pours Villa Mt. Eden Grand Reserve Chardonnay, Pinot Noir, and vineyard-designated Zinfandels.

NEARBY ATTRACTIONS: Bothe-Napa State Park (hiking, picnicking, horseback riding, swimming Memorial Day–Labor Day); Culinary Institute of America at Greystone (cooking demonstrations); Silverado Museum (Robert Louis Stevenson memorabilia).

DOMAINE CARNEROS

DOMAINE CARNEROS
1240 Duhig Rd.
Napa, CA 94559
707-257-0101
www.domainecarneros.com

OWNERS: Champagne
Taittinger and Kobrand
Corporation.

LOCATION: Intersection of
Hwys. 121/12 and Duhig
Rd., 4 miles southwest
of town of Napa.

APPELLATION: Carneros.

HOURS: 10 A.M.–6 P.M. daily.

TASTINGS: $6–$10 per glass,
depending on variety;
$13.50 for sampler of
3 sparkling wines or
3 Pinot Noirs.

TOURS: Hourly, 10:15 A.M.–
4 P.M. Group tours for
10 or more by appoint-
ment include glass of
Domaine Carneros wine.

THE WINES: Pinot Noir,
sparkling wine.

SPECIALTIES: *Méthode
champenoise* sparkling
wine, Pinot Noir.

WINEMAKER: Eileen Crane.

ANNUAL PRODUCTION: 45,000
cases.

OF SPECIAL NOTE: Table
service available in salon or
on terrace with panoramic
views of Carneros region.
Cheese plates and caviar
available for purchase.
Wine and French-related
items sold in winery shop.

NEARBY ATTRACTION:
di Rosa Preserve (indoor
and outdoor exhibits of
works by contemporary
Bay Area artists); Napa
Valley Opera House (live
performances in historic
building).

An architectural tribute to its French heritage, the chateau that houses Domaine Carneros would look at home in Champagne, France. It dominates a hillside in the renowned Carneros region in southern Napa, prime growing area for the grape varieties that go into the best sparkling wine and sumptuous Pinot Noir. The opulent winery is approached by a long series of steps that climb to a grand entranceway. French marble floors, high ceilings, and decorative features such as a Louis XV fireplace mantel imbue the interior with a palatial ambience. Guests are welcome to order wines in the elegant salon, warmed by a fireplace on cool days, or on the terrace.

Established in 1987, Domaine Carneros is a joint venture between Champagne Taittinger of France and Kobrand Corporation. President Director-General Claude Taittinger led the extensive search for the ideal site for making world-class sparkling wine. The Carneros region's long, moderately cool growing season and the fog that mitigates the summer heat allow for slow, even ripening and perfect acidic balance in the Pinot Noir and Chardonnay grapes. Domaine Carneros farms three vineyards totaling 200 acres in the appellation.

Harvest at Domaine Carneros begins in mid-August, when workers head out to pick grapes before dawn. A delicate balance of sugar and acidity is required for the best sparkling wine. The fruit is immediately brought to the press for the gentle extracting of the juice. From that moment through vinification, each lot is maintained separately before the exact blend is determined. The sparkling wines are made in accordance with the traditional *méthode champenoise,* in which secondary fermentation takes place in the bottle, not the tank. The grapes for Pinot Noir are gathered a week or two after the sparkling wine harvest is complete, then are fermented for ten days. After this, the juices are siphoned off, and the fruit is gently pressed to extract the remaining juice. The resulting wine is aged in French oak barrels for up to ten months before bottling.

In charge of these elaborate procedures is president Eileen Crane, who worked at Domaine Chandon and later served as winemaker and vice president of Gloria Ferrer Champagne Caves in nearby Sonoma. This experience—combined with the vision she shares with Taittinger on how to produce the elegant and delicate, yet intense sparkling wines—made her the ideal choice for overseeing the planning and development of Domaine Carneros. Crane focuses on making the most of the winery's fortuitous combination of climate, California technology, and French expertise to create wines of great character.

DUCKHORN VINEYARDS

Even if you were led blindfolded into this winery, you would have a good chance of guessing its name. One clue is the large mural of a duck-filled marsh on the wall in the tasting room. Another is a collection of duck prints. Still stumped? Take a look at the numerous cases filled with antique hunting decoys in the form of blue-winged teal, mallards, and pintails, all displayed neatly on glass shelves.

Dan Duckhorn is actually a duck fancier, as coincidence would have it. Despite these decorative details, the emphasis is squarely on his winery's three Bordeaux varietals, the most notable of which is Merlot. Dan and Margaret Duckhorn, who had earlier been in the vineyard nursery business, traveled extensively in Pomerol and St. Emilion, the Bordeaux appellations where Merlot is king. They then decided to create their own version.

In 1976, the Duckhorns, along with ten other families, purchased the ten acres in St. Helena where the winery is now located. The first vintage of Duckhorn Merlot, in 1978, came from the esteemed Three Palms Vineyard a few miles up the Silverado Trail. Although Dan and Margaret Duckhorn also started making Cabernet Sauvignon that year and added Sauvignon Blanc in 1982, the winery is most often associated with the Merlots made from its estate vineyards and the Three Palms' grapes.

Over the next twenty-four years, Duckhorn Vineyards expanded its annual production from sixteen hundred cases to sixty-five thousand, but during that time, the winery lacked a bona fide tasting room. Finally, in the fall of 2000, Duckhorn debuted its new facility, a farm-style Victorian with a wraparound porch. Extensively planted with evergreen trees and shrubs, the surrounding gardens have a Mediterranean look, with lots of lavender and native grasses. There are so many fountains that visitors can hear gurgling water from virtually any of the wooden benches arranged throughout the property. Colorful camellias in winter and rhododendrons in early spring are followed by blooming roses and purple butterfly bushes that attract a plethora of beneficial insects. Comfortable rattan sofas and chairs beckon from the front porch.

Inside the contemporary tasting room, casement windows on three sides allow for cross breezes and views of the vineyards and the forested hills to the west. Visitors are comfortably seated and served at a variety of marble-topped tables set with mats, glasses, tasting notes, and even a spit bucket. They are also treated to a bird's-eye look at the mural of one of Dan Duckhorn's favorite duck-hunting haunts at the base of the Sutter Buttes.

DUCKHORN VINEYARDS
1000 Lodi Ln.
St. Helena, CA 94574
707-963-7108
welcome@duckhorn.com
www.duckhorn.com

OWNER: Duckhorn Wine Company.

LOCATION: 3 miles north of St. Helena at Silverado Trail.

APPELLATION: Napa Valley.

HOURS: 10 A.M.–4 P.M. daily.

TASTINGS: Walk-in and by appointment.

TOURS: By appointment.

THE WINES: Cabernet Sauvignon, Merlot, Sauvignon Blanc.

SPECIALTIES: Estate-grown and vineyard-designated wines.

WINEMAKER: Mark Beringer.

ANNUAL PRODUCTION: 65,000 cases.

OF SPECIAL NOTE: Bottle limits on some wines. Annual events include Spring Open House (May).

NEARBY ATTRACTIONS: Bothe-Napa State Park (hiking, picnicking, horseback riding, swimming Memorial Day–Labor Day); Bale Grist Mill State Historic Park (water-powered mill circa 1846); Culinary Institute of America at Greystone (cooking demonstrations); Silverado Museum (Robert Louis Stevenson memorabilia).

FAR NIENTE

FAR NIENTE
1350 Acacia Dr.
Oakville, CA 94562
707-944-2861
info@farniente.com
www.farniente.com

OWNER: Private partnership.

LOCATION: .9 mile west of Hwy. 29 off Oakville Grade.

APPELLATION: Oakville.

HOURS: 10 A.M.–4 P.M. Monday–Saturday.

TASTINGS: By appointment. $40 for 5 current releases and library wines.

TOURS: By appointment.

THE WINES: Cabernet Sauvignon, Chardonnay, late harvest Semillon/ Sauvignon Blanc.

SPECIALTIES: Napa Valley Chardonnay, Napa Valley (Oakville) Cabernet Sauvignon.

WINEMAKER: Stephanie Putnam.

ANNUAL PRODUCTION: 30,000 cases.

OF SPECIAL NOTE: Some library wines available only at winery. Tasting includes a proprietary wine, Dolce, a late-harvest white blend. Collection of prized and rare classic cars.

NEARBY ATTRACTIONS: Napa Valley Museum (winemaking displays, art exhibits).

Hidden away on a private road just up from the Napa Valley floor, Far Niente is secluded among thirteen acres of southern-style landscaping distinguished by a great variety of texture, foliage, and blossoms. Some one hundred Autumn Gold gingko trees border the entrance drive to the winery. Farther along, towering redwoods, acacias, dogwoods, and century-old cork oak trees form a living canopy. The Far Niente gardens are famed for their collection of more than 8,000 southern azaleas, the largest single planting of the variety in California. Throughout the property, quaint touches like shaded pathways, hand-fitted flagstone stairs, and stone bridges arching across ponds create a memorable setting.

Far Niente was founded in 1885 by John Benson, a San Franciscan whose wealth was made in real estate and silver mines. To design the winery, Benson hired Hamden McIntyre, the architect for other stone wineries of the time, including Greystone, which became the Christian Brothers winery and is now occupied by the Culinary Institute of America. Benson named his estate Far Niente, taken from the Italian phrase *dolce far niente,* "sweet to do nothing."

The winery prospered until 1919, when it was abandoned at the onset of Prohibition. It would remain untouched for the next sixty years, until a different kind of visionary arrived in the valley. Gil Nickel, a former guided-missile analyst with an agricultural background gleaned through his family's nursery business in Oklahoma, bought Far Niente in 1979 and crushed its first Chardonnay that same year. Three years later, the exquisitely restored winery produced its first Cabernet Sauvignon. Today, the winery continues to focus on these two varietals.

After more than twenty years of being open only to the wine trade, Far Niente began offering tours and tastings to the public by appointment in 2004. Visitors are welcomed in the winery's Great Hall, with its original stone walls, hardwood floors, and antiques. The tour departs from the Great Hall and includes the winery, a portion of Far Niente's 40,000 square feet of caves, the landscaped grounds, and a collection of rare and classic cars, before returning for the tasting. Guests are served the current-release Chardonnay, Cabernet Sauvignon, and Dolce (the dessert wine made by the sister winery of the same name), plus two library Cabernet Sauvignons, allowing them to get a taste of history in a bottle.

FLORA SPRINGS WINERY AND VINEYARDS

This winery's history is a cautionary tale of sorts: Be careful what you wish for. In 1977, Jerry and Flora Komes were looking for a place to relax and watch the grapes grow. Their search led them to the Napa Valley, which has countless porches with vineyard views. Even then, they weren't thinking of growing the grapes themselves, let alone making wine.

Then the couple saw the 1956 Louis M. Martini house in the western foothills. Louis had died three years previously, and the property was looking rather shabby. Two of the buildings, the 1888 Rennie Winery and the 1885 Charles Brockhoff Winery, were filled with bats, rats, and rattlesnakes. The place looked more like a ghost town than a potential residence, but it had the key ingredient: the very views that the Komeses desired. As Jerry Komes recalled, "Outside of a home, it had all the things we weren't looking for."

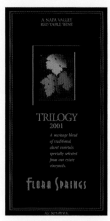

The couple bought the package and, inspired by the legacy of the land, decided to restore the property. Like so many other retirement projects, this one became a consuming passion that threatened the prospect of leisurely afternoons rocking on the porch. Before long, the property served as a magnet, luring two of Jerry and Flora's children. Son John, a general contractor and home winemaker, was fascinated by the challenges of producing wine and breathing life into the aged buildings. Daughter Julie and her husband, Pat Garvey, gave up careers in education, and Pat dedicated himself to learning the grape-growing business. Another son, Mike, also become a partner. After two vintages, John decided that he and Julie had pressed their luck as winemakers to the limit, and Ken Deis was hired. More than two decades later, he is still at it.

John's wife, Carrie, gets the credit for naming the new winery. There were two obvious life-giving sources to this venture, Flora herself and the continuously flowing springs that were the sole source of water for the property. Flora Springs had almost immediate success. The first commercially released wine, a Chardonnay, won a gold medal at the prestigious Los Angeles County Fair, the beginning of many awards for the winery.

Over the years, the family has acquired six hundred acres of vineyards in nine distinct Napa Valley locations, in addition to the original Komes Ranch. The winery sells 80 percent of these grapes to twenty-five premium wineries, which gives Flora Springs a unique opportunity to select the 20 percent that fits the winery's criteria. Visitors sample Flora Springs wines about a mile north of the actual winery at the tasting room, which has a rooftop deck.

FLORA SPRINGS WINERY AND VINEYARDS
677 Hwy. 29
St. Helena, CA 94574
707-967-8032
fswinery@aol.com
www.florasprings.com

OWNERS:
Komes/Garvey families.

LOCATION: About 1.5 miles south of downtown St. Helena.

APPELLATION: Napa Valley.

HOURS: 10 A.M.–5 P.M. daily (tasting room).

TASTINGS: $5 for 6 wines; $8 for 5 or 6 reserve wines.

TOURS: Of winery by appointment Monday–Friday afternoons.

THE WINES: Cabernet Sauvignon, Chardonnay, Merlot, Pinot Grigio, Pinot Noir, Sangiovese, Sauvignon Blanc, Trilogy (Meritage blend).

SPECIALTY: Trilogy.

WINEMAKER: Ken Deis.

ANNUAL PRODUCTION: 50,000 cases.

OF SPECIAL NOTE: Winery tour includes newly completed caves.

NEARBY ATTRACTIONS: Bothe-Napa State Park (hiking, picnicking, horseback riding, swimming Memorial Day–Labor Day); Bale Grist Mill State Historic Park (water-powered mill circa 1846); Culinary Institute of America at Greystone (cooking demonstrations); Silverado Museum (Robert Louis Stevenson memorabilia).

FREEMARK ABBEY WINERY

FREEMARK ABBEY WINERY
3022 St. Helena Hwy. North
P.O. Box 410
St. Helena, CA 94574
800-963-9698
wineinfo@freemarkabbey.
com
www.freemarkabbey.com

OWNER: Legacy Estates.

LOCATION: 2 miles north of
St. Helena at Lodi Ln.

APPELLATION: Napa Valley.

HOURS: 10 A.M.–5 P.M. daily
October–May; 10 A.M.–
6 P.M. June–September.

TASTINGS: $5 for 5 wines
(and tasting glass).

TOURS: By appointment.

THE WINES: Cabernet
Franc, Cabernet
Sauvignon, Chardonnay,
Edelwein Gold (late-
harvest Riesling), Merlot,
Petite Sirah, Port, Riesling,
Sangiovese, Viognier.

SPECIALTIES: Sycamore
Vineyards, Bosché Vine-
yards, and Napa Valley
Cabernet Sauvignons;
Edelwein Gold.

WINEMAKERS: Ted Edwards,
director of winemaking,
and Tim Bell.

ANNUAL PRODUCTION:
45,000 cases.

OF SPECIAL NOTE: Visitors
are welcome to picnic
at tables set on lawn.
Cabernet Franc, Petite
Sirah, Port, and Sangiovese
available only at winery.

NEARBY ATTRACTIONS:
Bothe-Napa State Park
(hiking, picnicking, horse-
back riding, swimming
Memorial Day–Labor
Day); Bale Grist Mill State
Historic Park (water-
powered mill circa 1846);
Silverado Museum
(Robert Louis Stevenson
memorabilia).

Of the many reasons people move to the Napa Valley and start a winery, the founder of Freemark Abbey may have had the most unlikely. Josephine Marlin Tychson, a native San Lorenzo, California, and her husband, John Tychson, a Danish immigrant, moved to St. Helena in 1881 in hopes that the region's climate would ameliorate John's tuberculosis. The couple, who had long wanted to make wine from their own vineyards, purchased acreage north of St. Helena for $8,500. They built their home on what later became known as Tychson Hill.

Using only a horse and plow, they began to expand their holdings by adding some ten acres of vines each year. John died in 1886, leaving Josephine to oversee the construction of a small winery that crushed 110 tons in 1890, producing Zinfandel, Riesling, and a Burgundy-style blend. Josephine Tychson was the first woman to build and operate a winery in California.

When an outbreak of the root louse *Phylloxera* began affecting her vineyards in 1893, Josephine sold the winery and some of her vineyards. The winery changed hands over the years, but the original wooden building survived until 1906, when it was replaced with one made of hand-cut stone from nearby Glass Mountain. In 1939, following Prohibition, three Southern Californians—Charles Freeman, Markquand Foster, and Albert "Abbey" Ahern—purchased the property and reopened the winery, combining parts of their names to come up with Freemark Abbey.

After a succession of other owners, a group of seven partners took over and resurrected the winery in 1967. Today, Freemark Abbey is making Riesling, as it did more than a century ago, but it is better known for its Cabernet Sauvignons and Chardonnays. The Cabernets from the Bosché and Sycamore vineyards were among the first wines in California to be named after specific vineyards. Another signature wine is the Edelwein Gold, a late-harvest Riesling. The tasting room is at the far end of a suspended walkway tucked into the back of a parking area conveniently located between a restaurant and a brew pub. The ideal place to savor wine is on a stone patio behind the tasting room, in the shade of market umbrellas.

GRGICH HILLS CELLAR

Few people driving along Highway 29 recognize both of the red, white, and blue flags flying in front of this winery. They certainly know one, the American flag. The other represents Croatia, the native country of winemaker and co-owner Miljenko "Mike" Grgich.

The simple red-tile-roofed, white stucco building may not be as flashy as those of nearby wineries, but as the saying goes, it's what's inside that counts. Once visitors pass beneath the grape-vine trellis and into the dimly lit recesses of the tasting room, they forget about exterior appearances. The comfortable, old-world atmosphere at Grgich Hills Cellar is not a gimmick.

The winery was founded by Mike Grgich (pronounced GUR-gitch) and Austin E. Hills on July 4, 1977. Both were already well known. Hills is a member of the Hills Brothers coffee family. Grgich was virtually notorious, drawn worldwide attention in "Paris Tasting," an all-French Chateau Montelena Chardonnay dies in a blind tasting. It was a fornia wine industry in general who was already acknowledged as

especially in France. He had 1976, when, at the now-famous panel of judges chose his 1973 over the best of the white Burgun-momentous occasion for the Cali-and in particular for Mike Grgich, one of the state's top winemakers.

Finally in a position to capitalize on his fame, Grgich quickly found a simpatico partner in Hills, who had a background in business and finance and was the owner of established vineyards. The two men shortly began turning out the intensely flavored Chardonnays that remain the flagship wines of Grgich Hills Cellar.

Grgich, easily recognizable with his trademark black beret, was born in 1923 into a winemaking family on the Dalmatian coast of Croatia. He arrived in California in 1958 and spent his early years at Beaulieu Vineyard, where he worked with the late, pioneering winemaker André Tchelistcheff before moving on to Mondavi and Chateau Montelena. Grgich continues to make wine and relies on a younger generation—daughter Violet Grgich, vice president of sales and marketing, and nephew Ivo Jeramaz, vice president of production and vineyard development—to carry on the family tradition. Visitors may well run into family members when taking the exceptionally informative winery tour or while sampling wines in the cool, cellarlike tasting room or in the newly built VIP tasting room and hospitality center.

GRGICH HILLS CELLAR
1829 St. Helena Hwy.
Rutherford, CA 94573
800-532-3057
info@grgich.com
www.grgich.com

OWNERS: Miljenko "Mike" Grgich and Austin Hills.

LOCATION: About 3 miles south of St. Helena.

APPELLATION: Napa Valley.

HOURS: 9:30 A.M.–4:30 P.M. daily.

TASTINGS: $5 for 5 wines.

TOURS: 11 A.M. and 2 P.M. weekdays; 11 A.M. and 1:30 P.M. weekends and holidays; all tours by appointment.

THE WINES: Cabernet Sauvignon, Chardonnay, Fumé Blanc, Merlot, Violetta (late-harvest dessert wine), Zinfandel.

SPECIALTY: Chardonnay.

WINEMAKER: Mike Grgich.

ANNUAL PRODUCTION: 80,000 cases.

OF SPECIAL NOTE: Barrel tastings held 2–4 P.M. on Friday afternoons in summer. Napa Valley Wine Train stops at Grgich for special tour and tasting; call 800-427-4124 for schedule.

NEARBY ATTRACTIONS: Bothe-Napa State Park (hiking, picnicking, horse-back riding, swimming Memorial Day–Labor Day); Bale Grist Mill State Historic Park (water-powered mill circa 1846); Silverado Museum (Robert Louis Stevenson memorabilia).

HALL NAPA VALLEY

HALL NAPA VALLEY
401 Hwy. 29 South
St. Helena, CA 94574
866-667-HALL (4255)
info@hallwines.com
www.hallwines.com

OWNERS: Craig and
Kathryn Hall.

LOCATION: 1.5 miles north
of Rutherford.

APPELLATION: Napa Valley.

HOURS: 10 A.M.–5:30 P.M.
daily.

TASTINGS: $8 for 4 Hall
wines; $7 for 2 Kathryn
Hall Vineyards wines.

TOURS: By appointment.

THE WINES: Cabernet Franc,
Cabernet Sauvignon,
Merlot, Sauvignon Blanc.

SPECIALTIES: Bordeaux
varietals.

WINEMAKER:
Mike Reynolds.

ANNUAL PRODUCTION:
6,000 cases.

OF SPECIAL NOTE: Visitors
can purchase gourmet
takeout food next door
at Dean & Deluca for a
picnic on winery grounds.

NEARBY ATTRACTIONS:
Silverado Museum
(Robert Louis Stevenson
memorabilia); Bothe-
Napa State Park (hiking,
picnicking, horseback
riding, swimming
Memorial Day–Labor
Day); Bale Grist Mill State
Historic Park (water-
powered mill circa 1846);
Culinary Institute of
America at Greystone
(cooking demonstrations).

The snappy red awning above the entry to the Hall Napa Valley winery catches the eye of motorists along busy Highway 29. Numerous splashes of red beckon from both the gardens and the modern sculptures in front of the tasting room, which opened in 2003 to offer Bordeaux varietals in a small building on a historic winery property.

The most imposing work of art in the entrance courtyard is a seven-foot-tall sculpture, *Moebus Tower*, by Texas artist Michelle O'Michael. Its form—a horizontal figure eight—represents the symbol for infinity. Painted a vibrant red, it inspired the color of the winery's logo. The winery commissioned several wine-related sculptures, including *Baccus* (a figure eating grapes) and *Toasters* (a couple toasting in a lavender flower bed), for display on the front and side walkways. Additional sculptures by contemporary artists adorn the tasting room, as well as the lawn in back of the winery, forming an outdoor gallery where guests can relax and enjoy unimpeded views of the Mayacamas Range to the west. Extensive plantings of penstemon, lavender, miniature roses, and other perennials create a lush garden setting, especially around the arbor-covered courtyards.

The original stone winery next door to the tasting room was built in 1885 by New England sea captain William Peterson. Over the next century, several owners put their own stamp on the winery, most notably the Napa Valley Cooperative Winery, a major producer in the 1930s. After Craig and Kathryn Hall took possession in 2003, they completely revamped the tasting room, which was built in the 1980s, transforming it into a colorful, airy space further brightened by original artwork from their personal collection.

Kathryn Hall, a former U.S. ambassador to Austria, was no stranger to the wine business when she bought her first Napa Valley vineyard in 1995. Her family had owned sixty-three acres of vineyards in Mendocino County, which she inherited and managed until 1992. By that time, she had taken vineyard management classes at the University of California at Davis, raised two children, and met and married Texas financier Craig Hall. Since then, the couple has acquired nearly three hundred acres of vineyards in Sonoma and Napa. Their holdings include Kathryn Hall Vineyards, a private winery in Rutherford, as well as the thirty-three-acre Hall Napa Valley winery, with its fourteen acres of vineyards.

Today, the Halls' properties in the Napa and Alexander valleys produce four Bordeaux varietals, Cabernet Franc, Cabernet Sauvignon, Merlot, and Sauvignon Blanc, under the Hall label. In the tasting room, they are served in Riedel crystal stemware, as befits the gallery setting.

HEITZ WINE CELLARS

Most travelers interested in sampling Heitz wines will visit the tasting room that opened in the spring of 2002 at the original winery site. Palms, traditional symbols of hospitality, greet visitors turning off the highway toward the native-stone building. The parking area is landscaped with Mexican sage, star jasmine, and long-blooming perennials. Demonstration vineyards have been planted in front of the entry doors. Inside, the mahogany floors, cabinets, and long, low tasting bar make for a sophisticated space. Visitors are welcome to amble out to the rear patio, where they find bench seating in the shade of a pergola. The winery's original vineyards, still in use, are just fifteen feet away.

Joe and Alice Heitz met in California in the 1940s. The couple headed north, and while Alice worked in Sacramento, Joe pursued degrees in enology at the nearby University of California at Davis. Joe Heitz, widely considered a winemaker's winemaker, honed his craft at a few wineries, notably Beaulieu Vineyards, where he spent seven years as understudy to acclaimed winemaker André Tchelistcheff.

Joe and Alice Heitz purchased their first vineyard and winery in 1961. Before long, they outgrew the eight acres and moved to the present 160-acre residence and ranch on Taplin Road, two miles due east from the current tasting room, at the end of a country lane in what locals call Spring Valley. The original winery became the first tasting room, then was replaced by the structure visitors see today. The Taplin Road property was first developed as a winery and vineyard in the 1880s by the Swiss-Italian family of Anton Rossi. Old oaks, rosebushes, wisteria, shaded benches, a couple of small farmhouses, and a beautiful 1898 stone cellar make parts of the ranch look more like a movie set than a working winery. Today, a second generation—winemaker David Heitz and president Kathleen Heitz Myers—oversees the winery's various Napa Valley ranches, which include 360 acres of vineyards.

The most famous wines Heitz makes come from three prestigious Napa Valley Cabernet vineyards: Bella Oaks Vineyard, Trailside Vineyard, and Martha's Vineyard. Perhaps no other vineyard name in the United States is as widely recognized as Martha's Vineyard in Oakville. Owned by the Tom and Martha May family, the thirty-four-acre property produces Cabernet Sauvignon known for its minty characteristics, rich flavors, and overall balance. Heitz Cellars receives all the grapes from the vineyard. So distinctive is the product that in 1966 Joe Heitz began to bottle it separately from his Heitz Napa Valley Cabernet, starting the widespread trend of vintners acknowledging specific vineyards whether they owned them or not.

HEITZ WINE CELLARS
Tasting Room:
436 St. Helena Hwy. South
St. Helena, CA 94574
707-963-2047
Winery:
500 Taplin Rd.
St. Helena, CA 94574
707-963-3542
www.heitzcellar.com

OWNERS: Heitz family.

LOCATION: 2.5 miles south of St. Helena (tasting room).

APPELLATION: Napa Valley.

HOURS: 11 A.M.–4:30 P.M. daily (tasting room).

TASTINGS: Complimentary.

TOURS: Of winery by appointment.

THE WINES: Cabernet Sauvignon, Chardonnay, Grignolino, Grignolino Rosé, Port, Zinfandel.

SPECIALTIES: Vineyard-designated Cabernet Sauvignons.

WINEMAKERS: David Heitz and Joe Norman.

ANNUAL PRODUCTION: 38,000 cases.

OF SPECIAL NOTE: Only producer of Italian variety of Grignolino in Napa Valley.

NEARBY ATTRACTIONS: Bothe-Napa State Park (hiking, picnicking, horseback riding, swimming Memorial Day–Labor Day); Bale Grist Mill State Historic Park (water-powered mill, circa 1846); Culinary Institute of America at Greystone (cooking demonstrations); Silverado Museum (Robert Louis Stevenson memorabilia).

MARKHAM VINEYARDS

MARKHAM VINEYARDS
2812 St. Helena Hwy. North
St. Helena, CA 94574
707-963-5292
www.markhamvineyards.
com

OWNER:
Mercian Corporation.

LOCATION: 1 mile north of
St. Helena on Hwy. 29.

APPELLATION: Napa Valley.

HOURS: 10 A.M.–5 P.M. daily.

TASTINGS: $3 for 3 white
wines; $5 for 4 red wines.

TOURS: By appointment.

THE WINES: Cabernet
Sauvignon, Chardonnay,
Merlot, Petite Sirah,
Pinot Noir, Reserve
Merlot, Sauvignon
Blanc, Zinfandel.

SPECIALTIES: All wines.

WINEMAKER: Kimberlee
Jackson Nicholls.

ANNUAL PRODUCTION:
150,000 cases.

OF SPECIAL NOTE: Pinot
Noir available only at
winery. Craft exhibits,
book signings, and art
exhibit openings in
summer months. Food-
and-wine-pairing
sessions ($35).

NEARBY ATTRACTIONS:
Bothe-Napa State Park
(hiking, picnicking, horse-
back riding, swimming
Memorial Day–Labor
Day); Bale Grist Mill State
Historic Park (water-
powered mill circa 1846);
Culinary Institute of
America at Greystone
(cooking demonstrations);
Silverado Museum
(Robert Louis Stevenson
memorabilia).

Few people are surprised to hear that Charles Krug, Schramsberg, and Sutter Home wineries were in business in 1874. Less widely known is that they were the only three wineries operating in the Napa Valley that year, when Jean Laurent founded the St. Helena winery that, less than a century later, would become known as Markham Vineyards.

Laurent, a Frenchman from Bordeaux, arrived in California in 1852, drawn by the lure of the 1849 Gold Rush. When his prospecting failed to pan out, he made his way to the city of Napa in 1868 and began growing vegetables. Laurent quickly assessed the high quality of the soil and, being from Bordeaux, realized the Napa Valley was ideally suited to grapevines. Six years later, he established the Laurent Winery in St. Helena.

After Laurent died in 1890, the property changed hands a number of times. In 1977, it was purchased by Bruce Markham, who had already acquired prime vineyard land on the Napa Valley floor, including 93 acres in Yountville once owned by Inglenook. By 1978, he had added the Calistoga Ranch at the head-lands of the Napa River and the Oak Knoll Vineyard in the Oak Knoll District. Altogether, the Markham estate vineyards now cover 330 acres, including the most recent acquisition, Trubody Vineyards, west of Yountville in the center of the valley. These four areas have distinct microclimates that contribute to the complexity of the various wines produced by the winery.

In 1988, the winery and vineyard holdings were sold to Japan's oldest and largest wine company, Mercian Corporation. Despite these changes, many things have remained constant. The current owners have maintained the winery's dedication to producing ultrapremium wines sold at relatively modest prices. The first employee hired by Markham, Bryan Del Bondio, is now president of Markham Vineyards, and Jean Laurent's original stone cellar sits at the heart of the facility.

Stylistically, the winery combines both historic and modern elements, with its old stone and concrete facade, and its subdued red metal roofing supported by round wooden columns. Lily ponds flank the approach to the tasting room, and beyond them, orange and yellow canna lilies provide bursts of color when the plants bloom in spring and summer. The tasting room has an atrium with a large fireplace that warms the huge space on cold days. Displayed throughout are fine art and crafts, from blown-glass torches, to jewelry and Limoges boxes, to hand-decorated ceramic plates, urns, and candlesticks. One side of the tasting room is devoted to changing exhibits by noted artists.

MERRYVALE VINEYARDS

On a bright day, it takes a moment for your eyes to adjust to the soft light of Merryvale's warm and spacious visitor center. Even so, it's impossible to miss the grand sight of the Historic Cask Room just inside the entrance, located behind wrought-iron doors worthy of a castle. Century-old, 2,000-gallon oak casks line the two-story stone walls and are as impressive as the long, massive table lit by candles that seats more than a hundred people. With its rich wood and exposed beam ceilings, the Cask Room is renowned for the private events and the winery's seasonal dinners.

Merryvale was founded in 1983, relatively recently compared to the stone structure it occupies, which has a storied past as the first winery to be built in the Napa Valley following Prohibition. Now completely renovated with honey-colored woods, the tasting room is part and parcel of a working winery. Visitors occasionally have to step aside to make way for a forklift skittering by with French oak barrels filled with Profile, Merryvale's flagship red Bordeaux-style blend.

The winery is located in one of Napa's prime grape-growing neighborhoods, and from the beginning, its mission has been to craft wines on par with the best in the world. To that end, along with its own vineyards, Merryvale has long-term contracts with a number of established growers from some of the finest vineyards in the valley. Three of Merryvale's wines come from Beckstoffer family grapes, which are held in such high regard that the vineyards are given equal billing on the label. In addition to sources in the heart of the Napa Valley, Merryvale obtains grapes from the Carneros appellation to the south, where the cooler climate allows early-ripening varietals such as Merlot to mature slowly and fully.

Merryvale's estate vineyards include acreage on the ridgetop east of St. Helena and at the historic Stanly Ranch in Carneros. At the former, Bordeaux varietals such as Cabernet Sauvignon, Cabernet Franc, and Petit Verdot are planted at an elevation of 1,100 feet and overseen by David Abreu, one of the top vineyard managers in the Napa Valley. The Carneros vineyard is planted in Chardonnay. Following traditional European methods, all of Merryvale's white wines are fermented and aged in French oak barrels, and all the red wines are aged in French oak barrels as well.

The Jack W. Schlatter family, which owns Merryvale, now has a second generation at the winery. Son René, who lives in St. Helena with his wife and two daughters, is executive vice president, carrying on the European traditions of his heritage.

MERRYVALE VINEYARDS
1000 Main St.
St. Helena, CA 94574
800-326-6069, ext. 439
info@merryvale.com
www.merryvale.com

OWNERS: Jack W. Schlatter and Family.

LOCATION: 1 block south of downtown St. Helena.

APPELLATION: Napa Valley.

HOURS: 10 A.M.–6:30 P.M. daily.

TASTINGS: $5 for Classic wines, $7 for reserve wines, $12 for Prestige wines.

TOURS: By appointment; also included with weekend seminars.

THE WINES: Cabernet Sauvignon, Chardonnay, Merlot, Pinot Noir, Muscat de Frontignan, Sauvignon Blanc, Syrah, Zinfandel.

SPECIALTIES: Profile (red Bordeaux-style blend) and Silhouette Chardonnay.

WINEMAKER: Stephen Test.

ANNUAL PRODUCTION: 75,000 cases.

OF SPECIAL NOTE: Wine seminars ($15) every Saturday and Sunday morning, by reservation (phone or online). Drop-in barrel tastings ($3) second Saturday and Sunday of every month. Seasons of the Napa Valley wine dinners in Historic Cask Room several times a year.

NEARBY ATTRACTIONS: Bothe-Napa State Park (hiking, picnicking, horseback riding, swimming Memorial Day–Labor Day); Culinary Institute of America at Greystone (cooking demonstrations); Silverado Museum (Robert Louis Stevenson memorabilia).

MUMM NAPA

MUMM NAPA
8445 Silverado Trail
Rutherford, CA 94573
707-967-7700
mumm_club@
mummnapa.com
www.mummnapa.com

OWNER: Allied Domecq
Wines USA.

LOCATION: East of
Rutherford, 1 mile south
of Rutherford Cross Rd.

APPELLATION: Napa Valley.

HOURS: 10 A.M.–5 P.M. daily.

TASTINGS: 3 half flutes for
$8 and up; $8–12 for
reserve wines.

TOURS: Hourly, 10 A.M.–
3 P.M.

THE WINES: Blanc de
Blancs, Blanc de Noirs,
Brut Prestige, Demi Sec,
DVX, Sparkling Pinot
Noir, Vintage Reserve.

SPECIALTY: Sparkling wine
made in traditional French
style.

WINEMAKER:
Ludovic Dervin.

ANNUAL PRODUCTION:
200,000 cases.

OF SPECIAL NOTE: Limited
availability of Chardonnay,
Pinot Gris, and Pinot Noir,
and of large-format
bottles, at winery.

NEARBY ATTRACTIONS:
Napa Valley Museum
(winemaking displays,
art exhibits).

For connoisseurs of champagne, relaxing outdoors on a sunny day with a glass of bubbly, good friends, and a vineyard view may be the ultimate pleasure. This is obviously what the founders of Mumm Napa had in mind when they conceived of establishing a winery in North America that could produce a sparkling wine that would live up to Champagne standards.

In 1979, representatives of Champagne Mumm of France and Joseph E. Seagram and Sons of New York began quietly searching for the ideal location for a winery. So secretive was their project that they even had a code name for it: Project Lafayette. The point man was the late Guy Devaux, a native of Epernay, the epicenter of France's Champagne district and an expert on *méthode champenoise.* In this French  style of winemaking, the wine undergoes its bubble-producing fermentation in the very bottle from which it will be drunk. Devaux criss-crossed the United States for four years before settling on Napa Valley, the country's best-known appellation.

The best way to appreciate Mumm Napa is to start with a tour. The winery has a reputation for putting on one of the best in the business, covering the complicated steps necessary to get all those bubbles into each bottle. The best time of year to take the tour is during the harvest season, usually between mid-August and mid-October. However, there is a lot to see at any time of year, and conveniently, the entire tour takes place on one level.

Visitors enter the winery through the wine shop; the tasting veranda is just beyond, with spectacular views of the vineyards and the Mayacamas Range.

Mumm Napa is also noted for its commitment to fine art photography. The winery exhibits the work of many renowned, as well as local, photographers in its expansive galleries. Guests may explore the Photography Galleries at their leisure, even while they enjoy a glass of sparkling wine. Most notable is the private collection of Mathew Adams, grandson of photographer Ansel Adams, on display in the exhibition gallery.

NICKEL & NICKEL

From the outside, the Nickel & Nickel winery is a charming, well-kept Napa Valley farm dating from the late nineteenth century. Yet, a closer look reveals that the farmstead facade camouflages a stunning, state-of-the-art winery that was designed exclusively to produce 100 percent varietal, single-vineyard wines.

Indeed, some of the buildings have been standing since the 1880s, when the surrounding land was settled by John C. Sullenger, the original landholder. This includes the stately farmhouse, featuring charming Queen Anne details, where visitors to Nickel & Nickel are welcomed. Restored in 2003 and named for its original owner, the Sullenger House is one of several restored buildings on the forty-two-acre estate that together capture the spirit of a nineteenth-century farm and create an architectural gem that mingles brand-new winemaking facilities with historic structures.

Visitors are met by the Sullenger House concierge and poured a glass of Chardonnay to enjoy in the living room. From the Sullenger House, the tour proceeds to the outbuildings where wine is made and stored. The only new building at Nickel & Nickel is the 5,800-square-foot fermentation barn, a post-and-beam structure fashioned from some 450 reclaimed, century-old fir beams. It was assembled using nineteenth-century techniques such as hand joinery for post-and-beam construction. From there, visitors are led down to the 30,000-square-foot underground cellar, which has groin arches and vaulted ceilings and can accommodate 3,200 French oak barrels.

The Sullenger House and farmstead buildings flank a traditional courtyard and are surrounded by eighty-year-old Sevillano olive trees and a white, three-rail fence. Extensive landscaping includes river birch, weeping willow, and Japanese maple trees, thirty-foot Canary palm trees, and a host of shrubs, perennials, and native plants. Guided sit-down tastings for a limited number of people are usually conducted in the dining room, or, depending on the time of year, tastings may also be held in the cellar, with its French tile floors and vaulted ceiling, or on the back porch.

The wine tastings include five of Nickel & Nickel's collection of 100 percent varietal, single-vineyard wines, all intended to express the distinct personality of each location. Except for a few select Sonoma vineyards, the wines come primarily from the Napa Valley. The sources range from eight acres in the Carpenter Vineyard in the Coombsville area of south Napa, to the small Dragonfly Vineyard in St. Helena, to thirty acres of clay loam soil in Sullenger Vineyard, the winery's home vineyard in Oakville.

NICKEL & NICKEL
8164 Hwy. 29
Oakville, CA 94562
707-967-9600
info@nickelandnickel.com
www.nickelandnickel.com

OWNER:
Private partnership.

LOCATION: On Hwy. 29 just north of Oakville Cross Rd.

APPELLATION: Oakville.

HOURS: 10 A.M.–3 P.M. Monday–Friday; 10 A.M.–2 P.M. Saturday-Sunday.

TASTINGS: By appointment. $30 for 5 wines.

TOURS: By appointment.

THE WINES: Cabernet Sauvignon, Chardonnay, Merlot, Syrah, Zinfandel.

SPECIALTIES: 100 percent varietal, single-vineyard wines.

WINEMAKER:
Darice Spinelli.

ANNUAL PRODUCTION:
20,000 cases.

OF SPECIAL NOTE: Bottle limits on some wines.

NEARBY ATTRACTIONS:
Napa Valley Museum (winemaking displays, art exhibits).

NIEBAUM-COPPOLA ESTATE WINERY

NIEBAUM-COPPOLA ESTATE WINERY
1991 St. Helena Hwy.
Rutherford, CA 94573
707-968-1100
800-RUBICON
info@niebaum-coppola.com
www.niebaum-coppola.com

OWNERS: Francis and Eleanor Coppola.

LOCATION: About 3 miles south of St. Helena via Hwy. 29.

APPELLATION: Napa Valley.

HOURS: 10 A.M.–5 P.M. daily; 10 A.M.–6 P.M., Friday and Saturday, Memorial Day–Labor Day.

TASTINGS: $15 for 4 wines; $30 for reserve wines (includes admission to grounds and museum).

TOURS: Chateau Tour ($15); Vineyard Tour ($25); Rubicon Tour ($50). Call 707-968-1177 for schedule.

THE WINES: Cabernet Franc, Merlot, Pennino Zinfandel, Rubicon; Director's Series Cabernet Sauvignon, Chardonnay, Merlot, Pinot Noir, Sauvignon Blanc, and Zinfandel.

SPECIALTY: Rubicon (Bordeaux blend).

WINEMAKER: Scott McLeod.

ANNUAL PRODUCTION: 325,000 cases.

OF SPECIAL NOTE: Film and historic memorabilia on display. Renting of model sailboats for sailing in pool. Shop including extensive tabletop and serving pieces and Italian olive oils and other condiments.

NEARBY ATTRACTIONS: Silverado Museum (Robert Louis Stevenson memorabilia); Napa Valley Museum (winemaking displays, art exhibits).

For newcomers to the wine scene, the name of film director and producer Francis Ford Coppola may overshadow that of Gustave Niebaum, but from a historical perspective, the two are on equal footing. For all visitors, a chance to taste wine in a chateau built in the 1880s is a rare treat in itself, but the displays devoted to the Niebaum and Coppola families, winemaking history, and movie memorabilia offer an opportunity not to be missed.

If someone made a film about this winery, the establishing shot would undoubtedly be a lingering look at Niebaum's massive stone Inglenook Chateau. Niebaum was a Finnish sea captain who used the fortune he acquired in the Alaska fur trade to establish his winery in 1879. He succeeded in creating an estate worthy of the ones he had visited in Bordeaux. Fast forward to the 1970s. After a series of corporate ownerships, the winery had lost its reputation, its label, and a lot of vineyard land that was sold off piecemeal. Enter Francis Ford Coppola, who, with his wife, Eleanor, began making wine at the old Niebaum winery in 1975. In 1995, they purchased the chateau and its adjacent vineyards, thereby reuniting the major parcels of the original estate.

Buying the property was just the beginning of Coppola's extensive project that, by 1997, restored and renovated the chateau and its grounds. In the European-style front courtyard, a redwood and stone pergola is graced with grapevines. Nearby, a ninety-by-thirty-foot reflecting pool is illuminated at night. During the day, children can rent elaborate wooden sailboats, reminiscent of those in the Luxembourg Gardens in Paris, to float in the shallow water.

Inside the chateau, the first thing visitors see is a grand staircase. Four master woodworkers labored for more than a year to build it from exotic hardwoods imported from Belize. At the top of the staircase is a large stained-glass window, Coppola's image of the reunification of this historic estate. In the second-floor museum, Don Corleone's desk and chair from *The Godfather,* costumes from Bram Stoker's *Dracula,* the 1948 car from *Tucker,* and Coppola's five Oscars are among the memorabilia on view. In the main lobby are two enormous tasting rooms where wines can be sampled at stand-up bars or at long tables. Also on the ground floor are displays of Coppola family photographs and mementos, as well as antique zoetropes and other artifacts from film history. Coppola pays homage to Niebaum not merely by giving him top billing. The Centennial Museum behind the staircase also relates the stories of the two immigrant families—Coppola is the son of Italian immigrants—who successfully pursued the American dream.

PEJU PROVINCE

Spotting Peju Province, even on a winery-lined stretch of Highway 29, is easy, thanks to a fifty-foot-tall tasting tower topped with a distinctive patinated copper roof. Although the tasting tower opened only in late 2003, the structure already looks weathered, as if it has been there for decades. Like the rest of the property, it could have been transplanted directly from the countryside of southern France.

The Rutherford estate had been producing wine grapes for more than eighty years when Anthony and Herta Peju bought it in 1983. They have been improving the thirty-acre property ever since, streamlining vineyard techniques and adding Merlot and Cabernet Franc grapes to the estate's core product, Cabernet Sauvignon. By the mid-1990s, demand for Peju Province wines outstripped supply. To satisfy it, the Pejus acquired a 350-acre property in northern Napa County in Pope Valley, planted a variety of grapes, and named it Persephone Vineyard, after a goddess in Greek mythology.

The Pejus entered the wine business by a somewhat circuitous route. Anthony Peju had been living in Europe when he was lured to Los Angeles by the movie industry, but then became interested in horticulture. After he met Herta Behensky, his future wife, he established his own nursery, yet secretly dreamed of owning a farm. The vibrant towns of the Napa Valley and their proximity to San Francisco's cultural attractions enticed him to search for vineyard property. A two-year quest ended in the purchase of what would become Peju Province.

Peju's horticultural experience, combined with his wife's talent for gardening, resulted in two acres of immaculately kept winery gardens. Together, they established a dramatic series of outdoor rooms linked by footpaths and punctuated with fountains and marble sculpture. Hundreds of flowering plants and trees create an aromatic retreat for the Pejus and their visitors. Lining both sides of the driveway are forty-foot-tall sycamore trees, their trunks adorned by gnarled spirals. Anthony Peju has trained the trees over the years. They will eventually create a living arch so that visitors will feel they are approaching the winery through a tunnel of green. Visitors reach the tasting room by crossing a small bridge over a koi-filled pool with fountains. An entrance door of Brazilian cherrywood is carved with the image of a farm girl blending water and wine. Inside the room, three muses gaze down from a century-old stained-glass window. This and an enormous seven-light chandelier illuminate the Turkish tile floors and the copper-and-steel railing that leads to the mezzanine, where a strategically placed circular window offers a garden view.

PEJU PROVINCE
8466 Hwy. 29
Rutherford, CA 94573
707-963-3600
800-446-7358
info@peju.com
www.peju.com

OWNERS: Anthony and Herta Peju.

LOCATION: 10 miles north of town of Napa on Hwy. 29.

APPELLATION: Napa Valley.

HOURS: 10 A.M.–6 P.M. daily.

TASTINGS: $5 for 4 or 5 wines (applicable to wine purchase).

TOURS: Self-guided or by appointment.

THE WINES: Cabernet Franc, Cabernet Sauvignon, Chardonnay, Merlot, Provence, Sauvignon Blanc, Syrah, Zinfandel.

SPECIALTIES: Rutherford Reserve Cabernet, Cabernet Franc, and Carnival, a French Colombard.

WINEMAKERS: Sean Foster and Anthony Peju.

ANNUAL PRODUCTION: 25,000 cases.

OF SPECIAL NOTE: Grape Stomping Party (September). Lush gardens. About 80 percent of wines available only at winery.

NEARBY ATTRACTIONS: Silverado Museum (Robert Louis Stevenson memorabilia); Napa Valley Museum (winemaking displays, art exhibits); Culinary Institute of America at Greystone (cooking demonstrations).

PINE RIDGE WINERY

PINE RIDGE WINERY
5901 Silverado Trail
Napa, CA 94558
800-575-9777
info@pineridgewine.com
www.pineridgewinery.com

OWNER: Pine Ridge Winery, LLC.

LOCATION: About 1.5 miles south of Yountville Cross Rd.

APPELLATION: Napa Valley.

HOURS: 10:30 A.M.– 4:30 P.M. daily.

TASTINGS: $10 for 3 current releases; $20 for 3 Cabernet Sauvignons (Rutherford, Stags Leap, and Andrus Reserve); $30 for Hillside Room tasting.

TOURS: By appointment, 10 A.M., 12 noon, and 2 P.M.

THE WINES: Cabernet Sauvignon, Chardonnay, Merlot.

SPECIALTY: Andrus Reserve.

WINEMAKER: Stacy Clark.

ANNUAL PRODUCTION: 55,000 cases.

OF SPECIAL NOTE: Guided, sit-down tastings in Hillside Room, a private cellar, by reservation.

NEARBY ATTRACTIONS: Napa Valley Museum (winemaking displays, art exhibits).

Situated in the heart of Napa Valley's Stags Leap District, Pine Ridge Winery could not have a more appealing setting—a romantic vale on a property bordered by thousands of multicolored Joseph's Coat roses. In 1978, when the winery was founded, it occupied a 50-acre estate that includes one of the oldest Chardonnay vineyards in the valley. Today, it has more than 220 acres of densely spaced vineyards in the Stags Leap District and four of the valley's other most renowned appellations—Carneros, Rutherford, Oakville, and Howell Mountain. Pine Ridge specializes in producing wines that embody the unique characteristics of the appellations in which its estate vineyards are located. The fusion of old-world traditions with innovative viticulture and winemaking practices yields powerful, yet balanced, Bordeaux-style red wines and Chardonnays that have consistently garnered critical acclaim.

Grapes from all of the Pine Ridge vineyards are harvested by hand and brought to the winery for processing. Then the wines are aged in caves that were excavated half a mile into the volcanic rock hillside and run 100 feet below ground level. An entrance to the caves is through glass doors on one side of the tasting room. Just beyond the doors is the Hillside Room, where sit-down tastings are offered to visitors by reservation.

PINE RIDGE

2000
Cabernet Sauvignon
Napa Valley – Stags Leap District
ESTATE GROWN, PRODUCED AND BOTTLED BY PINE RIDGE
WINERY, NAPA, CA • BW 5012 • ALC. 14.1% BY VOL. • 750ML

Visitors are greeted by a concierge, who escorts them to this private cellar, which affords a glimpse into the caves where some 4,400 French oak barrels are filled with aging wine. In this rarefied atmosphere, usually reserved for wine industry insiders, guests compare barrel samples with current releases and bottle-aged reserve wines. A wine educator guides the tasting and answers questions, while the guests sip wine and enjoy an accompanying selection of artisanal cheeses.

The wines served in the Hillside Room are crafted by winemaker Stacy Clark, who has been with Pine Ridge since 1983. She tastes samples from every block in each of the winery's sixteen vineyards, located throughout the Napa Valley.

After sampling the wines, visitors can learn more about vineyard management by taking a short walk from the tasting room to the Pine Ridge demonstration vineyards. Printed explanations detail grape-growing practices such as high-density, narrow-spaced planting, a method that decreases the grape yield per vine and thus intensifies fruit flavor.

PROVENANCE VINEYARDS

The grapes for Provenance's Rutherford Cabernet Sauvignon come from a vineyard that is part of the old Caymus Ranchero, which belonged to George Yount and, later, Thomas Rutherford. One of the area's earliest settlers, Yount arrived in 1838 and is believed to have been the first to plant wine grapes in Napa Valley. Nearby Yountville is named for him, just as Rutherford is named for Thomas Rutherford, who married one of Yount's granddaughters and received a portion of the ranch as a wedding present.

The property continued to change notable hands. Georges de Latour, founder of Beaulieu Vineyards, bought the vineyard in the early 1900s, and decades later, in 1988, well-known grape grower Andy Beckstoffer purchased it and proceeded to replant it with grapevines better suited to the local soil and growing conditions. It is a prized parcel, not simply because of its history but especially because of Rutherford's enviable loamy soil and a growing season characterized by hot, cloudless days and fog-cooled mornings and evenings.

Having chosen these premium grapes as the focus of its production, the founders of Provenance sought a facility in Rutherford. When a forty-five-acre property formerly occupied by another winery became available in the summer of 2002, the Chalone Wine Group did not hesitate to snap it up. Founding winemaker is Tom Rinaldi, who had spent twenty-two years making wine at Duckhorn Vineyards. At Provenance, he crafts Cabernet Sauvignon and Merlot for his longtime fans, using grapes from Napa's best subappellations for red wines.

By the time Provenance opened its doors in late 2003, the winemaking facility sported a fresh coat of Burgundy red paint, and the tasting room had been completely rebuilt. The first feature visitors notice in the tasting room is the floor made of old staves from barrel heads, which still bear legible coopers' marks. Lots of bare wood—on the walls and ceiling—and a horseshoe-shaped wood tasting bar create a clean look in keeping with the winery's displays of artwork by local artists. The white beamed ceiling and museum-quality lighting give the room the appearance of an art gallery.

The link between wine and art is underscored in the winery's name. *Provenance,* which rhymes with *Renaissance,* comes from a French term meaning origin or source. In the world of art, connoisseurs rely on provenance, the record of an artwork's ownership since its creation, as a guarantee of authenticity. At Provenance, the legacy of the vineyards and the quality of the esthetics attest to the authenticity of both the wine and the art.

PROVENANCE VINEYARDS
1695 Hwy. 29
P.O. Box 668
Rutherford, CA 94573
707-968-3633
info@provenancevineyards.com
www.provenancevineyards.com

OWNER: Chalone Wine Group.

LOCATION: About 3 miles south of St. Helena.

APPELLATION: Rutherford.

HOURS: 10 A.M.–4:30 P.M. daily.

TASTINGS: $10 for 4 wines ($5 applicable to purchase).

TOURS: By appointment.

THE WINES: Cabernet Sauvignon, Merlot, Sauvignon Blanc.

SPECIALTY: Rutherford Cabernet Sauvignon.

WINEMAKER: Tom Rinaldi.

ANNUAL PRODUCTION: 35,000 cases.

OF SPECIAL NOTE: Tours on slow days may include a barrel sampling that allows visitors to compare different unreleased vintages. Mount Veeder Merlot and Rutherford Sauvignon Blanc available only at winery.

NEARBY ATTRACTIONS: Bothe-Napa State Park (hiking, picnicking, horseback riding, swimming Memorial Day–Labor day); Bale Grist Mill State Historic Park (water-powered mill circa 1846); Culinary Institute of America at Greystone (cooking demonstrations); Silverado Museum (Robert Louis Stevenson memorabilia).

ROMBAUER VINEYARDS

ROMBAUER VINEYARDS
3522 Silverado Trail
St. Helena, CA 94574
800-622-2206
707-963-5170
www.rombauervineyards.com

OWNER:
Koerner Rombauer.

LOCATION: 1.5 miles north of Deer Park Rd.

APPELLATION: Napa Valley.

HOURS: 10 A.M.–5 P.M. daily.

TASTINGS: Complimentary, by appointment.

TOURS: By appointment.

THE WINES: Cabernet Sauvignon, Chardonnay, Merlot, Zinfandel.

SPECIALTY: Diamond Selection Cabernet Sauvignon

WINEMAKER:
Gregory Graham.

ANNUAL PRODUCTION:
50,000 cases.

OF SPECIAL NOTE: Zinfandel, Port, and Joy, a late-harvest Chardonnay, available only at winery. Tours include visit to barrel-aging cellar. Copies of the latest edition of *The Joy of Cooking* and other cookbooks by Irma Rombauer are available in the tasting room.

NEARBY ATTRACTIONS:
Bothe-Napa State Park (hiking, picnicking, horseback riding, swimming Memorial Day–Labor Day); Silverado Museum (Robert Louis Stevenson memorabilia); Culinary Institute of America at Greystone (cooking demonstrations).

The quarter-mile-long drive from the Silverado Trail leads to a winery ensconced in a forest of pine trees. On the far side of the low-slung building, a wide California ranch–style porch affords views that extend to the tree-covered ridge of the Mayacamas Range to the southeast. Without another structure in sight, the serene setting has the ambience of a fairytale kingdom secluded from the hustle and bustle of the valley floor. Directly below the winery, a gravel path winds down to a hill where roses are planted in the sun and azaleas thrive in the shade. Scattered about are a half-dozen metal sculptures of fantastical creatures such as a diminutive dinosaur and a life-size winged horse, all weathered to the point that they blend into the landscape.

The Rombauer family traces its heritage to another fertile wine area, the Reingau region in Germany, where Koerner  Rombauer's ancestors made wine. His great-aunt Irma Rombauer, wrote the classic book *The Joy of Cooking*. The tradition of linking wine to food is carried on today, with every member of the family involved in the daily operation of the winery, from selecting grapes to marketing the final product. K. R. (Koerner Rombauer III) and his sister, Sheana, are now in charge, respectively, of national sales and public relations.

Koerner Rombauer, a former commercial airline captain, and his late wife, Joan, met and married in Southern California, where both had grown up in an agricultural environment. Since they had always wanted their children to have rural childhood experiences similar to their own, they came to the Napa Valley in search of land. In 1972, they bought fifty acres and settled into a home just up the hill from where the winery sits today. Within a few years, they became partners in a nearby winery, which whetted their appetite for a label of their own and for making handcrafted wines with the passion and commitment of the family tradition. Taking advantage of the topography, the Rombauers built their family winery into the side of the hill. Rombauer Vineyards was completed in 1982.

By the early 1990s, the Rombauers realized they had the perfect location for excavating wine storage caves. Completed in 1997, the double-horseshoe-shaped cellar, extends for more than a mile into the hillside. Tours begin in the tasting room, which is personalized with an eclectic assortment of memorabilia from Koerner Rombauer's life. Among the more interesting items are the many signed photographs of famous people as diverse as test pilot Chuck Yeager, entertainer Barbra Streisand, former Secretary of State George Shultz, and country music star Garth Brooks, many of them with personal notes to Rombauer.

60

Welcome to
RUTHERFORD
HILL
Cave Tours · Tasting · Sales Daily from 10 to 5

RUTHERFORD HILL WINERY

Deep in a hillside east of the Silverado Trail lies a labyrinth of caves that extends nearly a mile. This subterranean facility is well suited for stashing thousands of barrels of wine that can age at fifty-eight to sixty degrees Fahrenheit and 85 percent humidity—ideal conditions for storing wine without the risk of evaporation that would occur in a less-humid environment. When the outside temperature spikes into the hundreds, all it takes is a major hosing down to set things right again.

A walk in the caves, which are redolent of red-wine aromas mingled with French and American oak, is a high point of a tour at Rutherford Hill. Built in 1984 at a cost of $1 million, the caves cover forty-four thousand square feet. They were the first ones in the Napa Valley created with mining technology rather than the hand labor used at other wineries during the nineteenth century.

Rutherford Hill is reached  by a narrow road leading up from the Silverado Trail to a dead end in front of what looks like an ultra-deluxe barn. The large redwood structure has a steep-sloping roof that extends nearly to the ground. Rough-hewn external support beams anchor it in the so-called Rutherford dust. Outside the tasting room, a dramatic two-story arbor of wisteria vines partially shades a large sunken courtyard in springtime. It was the Rutherford dust that attracted a series of owners who realized the fine, rust-colored soil bore similarities to that of Bordeaux's Pomerol region, home to some of the world's finest Merlot.

The "barn," built by renowned winemaker Joseph Phelps, houses the winery and tasting room. In 1976, the property was purchased by Bill Jaeger, whose late wife, Lila, was a pioneer in initiating Napa's olive oil craze. Olive oil is still made from the trees on the winery property. Jaeger converted the forty-acre vineyard on the hill below the winery to Merlot vines, which continue to produce grapes for the current owner, Anthony Terlato, who took over in 1996. Terlato and his family, realizing that growing their own grapes would be the key to creating consistently complex, high-quality wines, subsequently purchased 60 additional acres in the Rutherford District and also farm another 130 Napa acres under long-term contracts.

The Terlato family's involvement in the wine business began with Anthony's father, who owned one of Chicago's largest wine stores. Over time, Anthony Terlato became a leading importer and marketer of fine wines from around the world, including those from Rutherford Hill. Having their own winery was the next logical step in the family's marrying of smart business and the pleasures of a wine country lifestyle.

RUTHERFORD HILL WINERY
200 Rutherford Hill Rd.
Rutherford, CA 94573
707-963-1871
info@rutherfordhill.com
www.rutherfordhill.com

OWNER: Anthony Terlato.

LOCATION: About 2 miles south of St. Helena, just north of Rutherford Cross Rd. off Silverado Trail.

APPELLATION: Napa Valley.

HOURS: 10 A.M.–5 P.M. daily.

TASTINGS: $5 for 5 wines and logo glass; $10 for 5 reserve wines and logo glass.

TOURS: 11:30 A.M., 1:30 P.M., and 3:30 P.M. ($10); includes tasting of 5 wines and logo glass.

THE WINES: Cabernet Sauvignon, Chardonnay, Gewürztraminer, Merlot, Port, Sangiovese, Sauvignon Blanc, Zinfandel.

SPECIALTIES: Merlot, Port, Reserve Merlot, Zinfandel.

WINEMAKER: David Dobson.

ANNUAL PRODUCTION: 100,000 cases.

OF SPECIAL NOTE: Picnic areas with valley views. Wine-blending seminars. Some limited-production wines sold only at winery. Caves available for private rental. Lila Jaeger's extra-virgin olive oil and cookbooks by local authors carried at winery shop.

NEARBY ATTRACTIONS: Auberge du Soleil (hotel, restaurant); Silverado Museum (Robert Louis Stevenson memorabilia).

SILVER OAK CELLARS

SILVER OAK CELLARS
Napa Valley:
915 Oakville Cross Rd.
Oakville, CA 94562
Alexander Valley:
24625 Chianti Rd.
Geyserville, CA 95441
800-273-8809
info@silveroak.com
www.silveroak.com

OWNER:
Raymond T. Duncan.

LOCATION: Napa Valley:
1.2 miles east of Hwy 29;
Alexander Valley: 7 miles
from Canyon Rd. exit off
U.S. 101 via Chianti Rd.

APPELLATIONS: Napa Valley
and Alexander Valley.

HOURS: 9 A.M.–4 P.M.
Monday–Saturday.

TASTINGS: $10 (compli-
mentary glass included).
No reservations required.

TOURS: Monday–Friday,
1:30 P.M.; reservations
recommended.

THE WINE:
Cabernet Sauvignon.

SPECIALTY:
Cabernet Sauvignon.

WINEMAKER:
Daniel Baron.

ANNUAL PRODUCTION:
70,000 cases.

OF SPECIAL NOTE: Purchase
limits on some vintages.
Release days are held
simultaneously at both
estates for each wine:
Napa Valley Cabernet
on the Saturday closest
to February 1; Alexander
Valley Cabernet on
the Saturday closest to
August 1.

NEARBY ATTRACTIONS:
Napa Valley Museum
(winemaking displays,
art exhibits).

Fans of fine Cabernet Sauvignon line up hours in advance—sometimes even camping overnight—for the new release of each Silver Oak wine. The vigil has become something of a ritual for connoisseurs who want to be sure to take home some of the winery's hard-to-find bottles. During the early 1990s, on each semiannual release day in Napa Valley, just a handful of people waited for the winery doors to open, but as news of the extraordinary wine spread and the crowds grew larger, Silver Oak began serving espresso drinks and doughnuts to the early-morning crowds and passing hot hors d'oeuvres throughout the afternoon. Now each release day unfolds at both of the winery's estates, in Napa Valley and Alexander Valley, and many wine lovers plan vacations around the festive events.

The biggest attraction, of course, is what lies in the bottle. Silver Oak produces elegant Cabernet Sauvignons with fully developed flavors and seamless textures. The winemaking program combines meticulous vineyard practices, har- monious blending, and extensive aging in exclusively American oak barrels—followed by even more aging in bottles. When the wine reaches the consumer, it is a synergy of depth and delicacy.

The success of Silver Oak Cellars began with two visionary men, Ray Duncan and Justin Meyer. Duncan was an entrepre- neur in Colorado before being lured to California in the 1960s to help a friend work on a vine- yard deal. Impressed with the po- tential for wines in the Napa Valley and the Alexander Valley in Sonoma Valley, he purchased 750 acres of pastures, orchards, and vineyards within a year. In 1972, he formed a partnership with Meyer, a former Christian Brothers winemaker. The partners' work together lasted thirty years, until Meyer passed away in 2002.

Today the Duncan family sustains the commitment to excellence that has long been a hall-mark of Silver Oak Cellars. Each of the two estates is devoted to an individual style of Cabernet Sauvignon. The Alexander Valley wine has a particularly soft and fruity character, while the some-what bolder Napa Valley wine has firmer tannins, making it appropriate for longer cellar aging. Both estates welcome visitors and have tasting rooms where they can taste and compare the current release from each appellation. The Napa Valley winery, on the site of the old Keig Dairy in Oakville, features a massive stone building with a simple, but elegant, wood-paneled tasting room. The Alexander Valley winery has an airy tasting room and an inviting courtyard for relaxing and enjoying the leisurely pace of Sonoma County.

SILVERADO VINEYARDS

A steep, curving driveway, worthy of a ski slope, leads to the spectacular site of Silverado Vineyards. On either side of the road, wildflowers cling to the hillside as if for dear life. Yet nothing compares to the dramatic site of the winery itself, a vision in ocher and terra-cotta, stone and stucco, that brings Tuscany to mind. Many a visitor has noticed that Napa bears more than a passing resemblance to the Italian countryside.

In the mid-1970s, Diane Miller and her husband, Ron Miller, purchased two neighboring Napa Valley vineyards. "It was a beautiful land," she says, "and it was a land that was working." For the first few years, the Millers sold their grapes to local vintners, who made gold-medal-winning wines from them. Inspired by this success, they established Silverado Vineyards in 1981 and started construction on their own winery,  which opened to the public for tours and tastings in 1987. The Millers named their new winery after the long-vanished mining community that once thrived on the slopes of nearby Mount St. Helena. The name Silverado was made famous by author Robert Louis Stevenson, who lived there in the 1880s and wrote about the region in *The Silverado Squatters*.

Since Silverado was founded, the winery has acquired additional vineyards that it farms itself. Some of those vineyards, notably ninety-five acres of Cabernet Sauvignon and Merlot, are visible from the second-floor visitors' center. Guests can sip their wine on a terrace paved with cobblestones that once graced New York City streets. If you look closely, you can see that some of the stones are worn smooth, while others are set bottom side up, with their still-rough surfaces showing. Only a low wall separates the terrace from the abundant vines and wildflowers that bloom throughout the seasons.

The adjacent, spacious tasting room opened in 2000, replacing the much smaller original tasting room in another part of the building. French doors offer north-facing panoramas of vineyards and the hilly Stags Leap landscape. Huge antique beams of Douglas fir, imported from a lumber mill in British Columbia, span the ceiling. Overall, the design is grand but simple, recalling a Tuscan villa. Across the hall, double doors provide a view of a temperature-controlled barrel cellar. There is no access to the cellar from here, but visitors are invited to open the doors and inhale the heady aroma.

While the winery has grown a bit over the years, Silverado's winemaking staff still believe that small is a good way of doing things. From hand harvesting, to small lot fermentation, to use of French oak barrels, visitors are able to see each step in the winemaking process.

SILVERADO VINEYARDS
6121 Silverado Trail
Napa, CA 94575
707-257-1770
info@silveradovineyards.com
www.silveradovineyards.com

OWNERS: Miller family.

LOCATION: About 2 miles east of Yountville.

APPELLATION: Napa Valley.

HOURS: 10:30 A.M.–5 P.M. daily.

TASTINGS: $10 for 4 estate wines. Reserve and library tastings available.

TOURS: By appointment.

THE WINES: Cabernet Sauvignon, Chardonnay, Merlot, Sangiovese, Sauvignon Blanc.

SPECIALTIES: Limited Reserve Cabernet Sauvignon, Chardonnay, Merlot.

WINEMAKERS: Jon Emmerich and Jack Stuart.

ANNUAL PRODUCTION: Unavailable.

OF SPECIAL NOTE: Limited-production wines available only in tasting room.

NEARBY ATTRACTIONS: Napa Valley Museum (winemaking displays, art exhibits); COPIA: The American Center for Wine, Food and the Arts.

SPRING MOUNTAIN VINEYARD

SPRING MOUNTAIN VINEYARD
2805 Spring Mountain Rd.
St. Helena, CA 94574
707-967-4188
office@springmtn.com
www.springmountain
vineyard.com

OWNER: J. E. Safra.

LOCATION: About 1.5 miles
northwest of downtown
St. Helena.

APPELLATION: Spring
Mountain District.

HOURS: 10 A.M.– 4 P.M.
Monday–Saturday.

TASTINGS: By appointment.

TOURS: By appointment.

THE WINES: Estate-bottled
Cabernet Sauvignon,
Sauvignon Blanc, Syrah.

SPECIALTIES: Elivette
Reserve Cabernet,
mountain-grown
Cabernet Sauvignon.

WINEMAKER: Jac Cole.

ANNUAL PRODUCTION:
10,000 cases.

OF SPECIAL NOTE: Tour
includes visit to winery's
extensive caves. Demon-
stration vineyard with
gobelet trellising system.
Displays of photography
and antique farm equip-
ment. Library selections
of Cabernet Sauvignon.
Large-format bottles
available.

NEARBY ATTRACTIONS:
Bothe-Napa State Park
(hiking, picnicking,
horseback riding, swim-
ming Memorial Day–
Labor Day); Bale Grist
Mill State Historic Park
(water-powered mill circa
1846); Culinary Institute
of America at Greystone
(cooking demonstrations);
Silverado Museum
(Robert Louis Stevenson
memorabilia).

Every tour of the historic Spring Mountain Vineyard concludes with a sit-down wine tasting in a picturesque 1885 Victorian called Miravalle. The crowning glory of the Miravalle estate, this 8,000-square-foot mansion was built by the original owner, Tiburcio Parrott, one of the most colorful of Napa Valley's many nineteenth-century characters. The winery closed to the public in 1992 so that the owner could focus on restoration and replanting the hillside vine-yards. It reopened in late 2003. The cream-colored house capped with a cupola boasts original ceilings, moldings, and inlaid wood floors. Another notable original feature is the stained-glass window with the bright green parrot on the first-floor landing. It may look familiar because the mansion was the fictional vintner's home on *Falcon Crest*, the popular 1980s television series.

The estate's real history is far more memorable than any soap opera. Spring Mountain Vineyard incorporates three properties that were producing wine in the late 1800s: Miravalle, Chateau Chevalier, and La Perla, site of the first Cabernet Sauvignon planting on Spring Mountain, in 1870. Even back then, grape growers and winemakers recognized the distinctive attributes of what is now known as the Spring Mountain District, namely, steep slopes and shallow soils that create such widely diverse conditions that Spring Mountain Vineyard has 130 identifiable vineyard blocks, each with a different elevation, exposure, and soil. Only 225 acres of the 845-acre estate have been planted—85 percent of them in classic red Bordeaux varieties: Cabernet Sauvignon, Cabernet Franc, Merlot, and Petit Verdot. Each year the winemaker captures the personality of the Spring Mountain Vineyard and the vintage in two blends, the Estate Cabernet blend and the reserve blend, Elivette.

Although the property changed hands over the past 120 years, it has been maintained or restored to look much as it did in the nineteenth century. Along with grapes, Parrott had planted some six thousand olive trees and hundreds of citrus trees and roses. To these, the current owner added dozens of banana, fig, palm, and exotic fruit trees. A tour also includes an elegant old shingled horse barn with a collection of antique winemaking equipment and other historical objects. A gal-lery displays photographs of nineteenth-century wine pioneers, including Tiburcio Parrott. Near the barn is a demonstration vineyard where visitors can view the winery's unusual "vertical gobelet" trellising system. Following this ancient method, each vine is shaped into a graceful goblet form resembling the glasses used for tasting red wines at Miravalle.

ST. CLEMENT VINEYARDS

Rows of vineyards march up the slope to a fetching olive-green structure that was obviously built as a private residence. Fritz H. Rosenbaum, a German stained-glass merchant, and his wife, Johanna, built this Gothic-Victorian–style home for their family in 1878. His plans included a properly equipped wine cellar where he could make wines as he had in the old country. Thanks to those first wines from the stone cellars beneath the house, Johannaberg Cellars became one of the earliest commercial wineries in the Napa Valley. Nearly a century and a half later, the original cellars are used to house some of the thirty thousand cases that St. Clement produces annually.

The pleasant walkway up from the parking lot is rimmed with towering white and pink oleander bushes, which give way to hydrangeas and roses. As an extra bit of charm, tiny blossoming ground-cover plants have gained toeholds in the crevices of the old stone retaining wall in front of the historic home.

The Rosenbaums situated their house to take advantage of a 180-degree view of the Vaca Range to the east. Visitors can enjoy the same vista from a charming swing on the front porch or from the stone patio nearby. Here small tables for two are set in the shade of fir and poplar trees. The patio is rimmed on two sides by a low stone wall and on the other two by a short, old-fashioned wrought-iron fence. In the center is a fountain encircled by fragrant star jasmine. The entire property would make a lovely restaurant if it weren't such a success as a winery.

St. Clement hasn't been a winery all these decades. After Fritz Rosenbaum's death in 1893, the grand residence was sold to the first of several families who lived in it until the middle of the twentieth century. By the 1940s, the house had fallen into disrepair. It was rehabilitated and restored in 1962 by Michael and Shirley Robbins, who established the property as Spring Mountain Vineyards in 1968.

The home changed hands again in 1975, when Dr. and Mrs. William Casey purchased it and christened their first wines St. Clement Vineyards. Their releases until 1979 consisted of small quantities of Cabernet Sauvignon and Chardonnay. Then they built a modern stone winery to accommodate up to ten thousand cases. Although the winery changed hands again and again, the Victorian remained a private home. In 1991, it was remodeled once more and welcomed the public to tastings and open houses. Eight years later, it was purchased by Beringer (now Beringer Blass Wine Estates). The specialty is still small lots of ultrapremium wines made from Napa Valley grapes.

ST. CLEMENT VINEYARDS
2867 Hwy. 29 North
St. Helena, CA 94574
800-331-8266
info@stclement.com
www.stclement.com

OWNER: Beringer Blass Wine Estates.

LOCATION: North side of St. Helena.

APPELLATION: Napa Valley.

HOURS: 10 A.M.–4 P.M. daily.

TASTINGS: $5 for 5 wines.

TOURS: By appointment.

THE WINES: Cabernet Sauvignon, Chardonnay, Merlot, Sauvignon Blanc.

SPECIALTY: Cabernet Sauvignon.

ANNUAL PRODUCTION: 30,000 cases.

OF SPECIAL NOTE: Picnic tables available by reservation only for parties of up to 15 people.

NEARBY ATTRACTIONS: Bothe-Napa State Park (hiking, picnicking, horseback riding, swimming Memorial Day–Labor Day); Bale Grist Mill State Historic Park (water-powered mill circa 1846); Culinary Institute of America at Greystone (cooking demonstrations); Silverado Museum (Robert Louis Stevenson memorabilia).

STERLING VINEYARDS

STERLING VINEYARDS
1111 Dunaweal Ln.
Calistoga, CA 94515
707-942-3344
800-726-6136
info@sterlingvineyards.com
www.sterlingvineyards.com

OWNER: Diageo Chateau &
Estate Wines.

LOCATION: Just south of
Calistoga between Hwy. 29
and Silverado Trail.

APPELLATION: Napa Valley.

HOURS: 10:30 A.M.–4:30 P.M.
daily.

TASTINGS: $15 for 4 wines
(includes aerial tram).

TOURS: Self-guided tours
available during operat-
ing hours. Groups by
appointment.

THE WINES: Cabernet
Sauvignon, Chardonnay,
Malvasia Bianca, Merlot,
Muscat Canelli, Pinot Gris,
Pinot Noir, Sangiovese,
Sauvignon Blanc, Syrah,
Viognier, Zinfandel.

SPECIALTIES: Vineyard-
designated Chardonnay,
Pinot Noir, Merlot, and
Cabernet Sauvignon; reserve
Chardonnay, Merlot, and
Cabernet Sauvignon.

WINEMAKER:
Rob Hunter.

ANNUAL PRODUCTION:
400,000 cases.

OF SPECIAL NOTE: Children are
given juice, crayons, and note-
cards to color. Annual events
include Merlot in May. Ten
wines made for Cellar Club
members available to general
public only at winery. Historic
collection of wine art and artifacts on display year-round.

NEARBY ATTRACTIONS: Bothe-
Napa State Park; Robert Louis
Stevenson State Park; hot-air
balloon rides; Old Faithful
Geyser of California; Petrified
Forest; Sharpsteen Museum
(exhibits on Robert Louis
Stevenson and Walt Disney
animator Ben Sharpsteen).

Travelers in the upper Napa Valley often get out their cameras as soon as they see the striking white buildings atop a three-hundred-foot forested knoll south of Calistoga. Even
more camera-worthy is the journey to the winery via aerial tram. Cars and worries are left
behind as visitors glide up the hill. The winery's designer, inspired by Napa's Mediterranean climate,
intentionally modeled Sterling on the style of architecture on the photogenic Greek island of Mykonos.

The winery also stands out for its self-guided tours, which allow visitors to explore the facility
from elevated platforms that feature educational graphics and a DVD video showing the entire
winemaking process. The tour culminates on a terrace offering a commanding view of the Napa
Valley. Upon entering the main tasting room, guests are greeted with a complimentary glass of
Sauvignon Blanc, then are shown to a table where the staff serves a choice
of current releases. Visitors can enjoy the comfortable surroundings,
or in warm weather sit on a patio with a view of the Bay Area's highest
mountain, 4,344-foot Mt. St. Helena. Displayed throughout the tasting
rooms is a collection of wine art and artifacts spanning five centuries.

Sterling was established in 1969 with the purchase of fifty vineyard acres by Englishman and inter- national paper broker Peter Newton.
In 2002, the winery completed a $14 million renovation, which included three new tasting
rooms—one for the public, another for reserve wines, and yet another for Cellar Club members.
Sterling has purchased a number of vineyards over the decades and now farms twelve hundred
acres in the Napa Valley. These properties vary widely in topography, soil types, and
microclimates, from the very steep Diamond Mountain Ranch west of Calistoga to the rolling hills
around Winery Lake in the southern Carneros near San Francisco Bay. The winery also acquires
grapes from other sources. One is the prestigious Three Palms Vineyard just southeast of the
winery and owned by Sloan Upton, Sterling's first vineyard manager, and his brother John. The
vineyard's stately palms were planted in the late 1800s by then-landowner Lilly Hitchcock Coit,
best known for building San Francisco's Coit Tower.

When the winery was established, the owners were confident about the future of Cabernet
Sauvignon, but took a chance on three then-unproven varietals—Sauvignon Blanc, Chardonnay,
and Merlot—by including them in early vineyard plantings. Consequently, in 1969, Sterling Vineyards became the first American producer of a vintage-dated Napa Valley Merlot.

SWANSON VINEYARDS AND WINERY

Time seems to stand still when you step inside the Swanson Salon. Or maybe the Salon takes you back to an earlier era of leisure, luxury, and lingering conversation. For one hour at least, visitors can forget the outside world and concentrate on the wine and their fellow tasters. Only eight people are seated at each tasting session. Surrounded by fine things and served one wine after another, visitors are guided by the "salonnier" through that day's menu of wines, accompanied by little plates of elegant cheeses and crackers and capped with a bonbon made exclusively for Swanson, paired with the final wine.

At the appointed hour, arriving visitors are welcomed by the host into the stucco winery with its weathered blue window shutters. The fantasy begins when they step into an intimate, intensely decorated room with coral-colored walls adorned by seventeen colorful paintings, some as tall as eight feet, by noted Bay Area figurative artist Ira Yeager. Together, they make up his *Vintage Peasant* series, most of the works having been created especially for this room. Then it is time to take a seat at an octagonal table made of Moroccan wood inlaid with agate. A small menu lists the day's offerings, which are already arranged on the table. Always among them are wines available only at the winery.

According to Alexis Swanson, director of marketing, the salon concept coalesced in 2000 as an expression of the Swanson family's affinity for an old-fashioned way of life. "It's all about service and intimacy and obsessive attention to detail," she says. "Every tasting is like a little cocktail party held in each guest's honor. The common thread is a love of wine, but the conversation is never technical. It's all a balance of humor and whimsy, art and theater." One look around the jewel box of a room proves Swanson's point. Details of the decor may change slightly over the years, but the style, established by noted New York interior designer Tom Britt, does not.

Catering to the traveler looking for the less attainable, the Salon offers such small-batch wines as Angelica, Rosato, Sangiovese, Syrah, Late-Harvest Semillon, Petite Sirah, and a sparkling Muscat—wines found only at the Swanson Salon.

SWANSON VINEYARDS AND WINERY
1271 Manley Ln.
Rutherford, CA 94573
707-967-3500
salon@swansonvineyards.com
www.swansonvineyards.com

OWNER: W. Clarke Swanson, Jr.

LOCATION: .5 mile west of Hwy. 29.

APPELLATION: Napa Valley.

HOURS: By appointment Wednesday–Sunday, 11 A.M., 1:30 P.M., and 4 P.M.

TASTINGS: $25 for 4 wines; $45 for 7 wines.

TOURS: None.

THE WINES: Alexis (Cabernet Sauvignon blend), Angelica, Late-Harvest Semillon, Merlot, Petite Sirah, Pinot Grigio, Rosato, Sangiovese, sparkling Muscat, Syrah.

SPECIALTIES: Alexis, Merlot.

WINEMAKER: Chris Phelps.

ANNUAL PRODUCTION: 25,000 cases.

OF SPECIAL NOTE: Number of guests limited to 8. Angelica, Muscat, Syrah, Rosato, Sangiovese, Late-Harvest Semillon, and Petite Sirah available only at winery.

NEARBY ATTRACTIONS: Silverado Museum (Robert Louis Stevenson memorabilia); Napa Valley Museum (winemaking displays, art exhibits).

TWOMEY CELLARS

TWOMEY CELLARS
1183 Dunaweal Ln.
Calistoga, CA 94515
800-505-4850
www.twomeycellars.com

OWNERS:
Duncan family.

LOCATION: 2 miles south of Calistoga at corner of Hwy. 29.

APPELLATION: Napa Valley.

HOURS: 9 A.M.–4 P.M. Monday–Saturday.

TASTING: $5 (includes complimentary wineglass).

TOURS: Available on a drop-in basis.

THE WINE: Merlot.

SPECIALTY: Merlot.

WINEMAKER: Daniel H. Baron.

ANNUAL PRODUCTION: 11,000 cases.

OF SPECIAL NOTE: The latest vintage is released each year in May and is available in limited quantity.

NEARBY ATTRACTIONS: Bothe-Napa State Park (hiking, picnicking, horseback riding, swimming Memorial Day–Labor Day); Robert Louis Stevenson State Park (hiking); hot-air balloon rides; Old Faithful Geyser of California; Petrified Forest; Sharpsteen Museum (exhibits on Robert Louis Stevenson and Walt Disney animator Ben Sharpsteen).

One of the very few wineries devoted to *soutirage traditional* winemaking, Twomey Cellars produces primarily Merlot. All of the grapes for the Merlot come from a single Napa Valley vineyard, the Soda Canyon Ranch. The focus on Merlot allows the winemaker to practice painstaking, time-honored techniques that maximize the inherent qualities of the grapes.

Twomey (pronounced "TOO-mee") Cellars opened the winery and tasting room in June 2003. They are located in the northern part of Napa Valley, just south of Calistoga on Highway 29. The sleek, but intimate, tasting room is housed in one of two matching clapboard cottages in front of the winemaking facility. The gleaming white buildings are surrounded by landscaped gardens and flourishing vineyards.

But it is the grapevines in the southeastern Napa Valley that provide the fruit for Twomey Cellars Merlot. The 145-acre Soda Canyon Ranch sits on deep volcanic soil and is tightly planted with French Merlot vines selected for their low yield of small, intensely flavored berries. The long, warm days in this area are perfect for ripening sugar levels, while the cool, foggy breezes from nearby San Pablo Bay extend the growing season without the risk of overripening the fruit.

Soda Canyon Ranch produces a particularly complex Merlot that warrants meticulous handling. Twomey winemaker Daniel Baron became well versed in the *soutirage traditional* approach used in Bordeaux when he spent a year working in Pomerol and St. Emilion. Few other California wineries apply this French technique to Merlot. Essentially, it is a slow, careful process whereby the wine is decanted from one barrel to another without the disruptive effects of a pump. This method, refined over centuries, remains the ideal way to clarify red wines to crystal-clear brilliance while drawing the fruit characteristics forward and softening the tannins.

The grapes are crushed and their juice fermented before being moved into thin-staved French oak barrels. During eighteen months of aging, the wine is racked five times, a process that removes the wine from the lees, or solid sediments, which fall to the bottom of the barrel. Each barrel has two reed-wrapped stoppers, called *esquives,* in its head. Following the *soutirage traditional* method, the cellar worker removes an *esquive* and replaces it with a bronze valve that allows the wine to flow by gravity or air pressure until he sees the first sign of sediment. He then stops the flow, leaving behind a small amount of cloudy wine. The clear wine is transferred into a second barrel, a method that preserves its full aromatic intensity and fosters a smooth, silky texture.

WHITEHALL LANE WINERY

Ocher and lavender, the colors of a California sunset, soften the geometric lines of Whitehall Lane, an angular, contemporary structure that stands in contrast to the pastoral vineyard setting. As if to telegraph the business at hand, the building's large windows have been cut in the shape of wine goblets. In front of the winery, a single row of square pillars runs alongside a walkway, each pillar supporting a vine that has entwined itself in the overhanging pergola.

Glass doors open into a tasting room that continues the overall theme with yellow walls, a white beamed ceiling, and a triptych painted with a stylized vineyard scene. The painting is a classic image that befits an estate where the first grapevines were planted in 1880. Even then, Napa Valley settlers were drawn to Rutherford's deep, loamy soils and sunny climate. A vestige of those early days, an old barn built for equipment storage, is still in use today.

In 1979, two brothers bought the twenty-six-acre vineyard and founded the winery they named after the road that runs along the south border of the property. They produced Merlot and Cabernet Sauvignon before selling the property nine years later. The Leonardini family of San Francisco took over the Whitehall Lane Estate in 1993. Tom Leonardini, already a wine aficionado, had been looking for property to purchase. He was aware of the winery's premium vineyard sources and some of its outstanding wines. Moreover, unlike his previous enterprises, the winery presented an opportunity to create a business that could involve his entire family.

Leonardini immediately updated the winemaking and instituted a new barrel-aging program. He also replanted the estate vineyard in Merlot and Sauvignon Blanc and began acquiring additional grape sources. Whitehall Lane now owns five Napa Valley vineyards, a total of 110 acres on the valley floor: the estate vineyard, the Rutherford West Vineyard, the Bommarito Vineyard, the Leonardini Vineyard, and the Glen Oak Vineyard. The wines produced from these vineyards have been rated among the top five in the world by *Wine Spectator* magazine. The 1995 Reserve Cabernet Sauvignon was the first to be selected for this honor, in 1998. Shortly thereafter, in 2000, the 1997 Reserve Cabernet Sauvignon was rated the world's number three wine, followed, in 2002, by the 1999 Cabernet Sauvignon Napa Valley as another top-five wine.

Tom Leonardini has succeeded in creating a family business that involves his wife as well as his five children, three of whom are directly involved in the winery's day-to-day operations.

WHITEHALL LANE WINERY
1563 Hwy. 29
St. Helena, CA 94574
800-963-9454
greatwine@whitehalllane.com
www.whitehalllane.com

OWNER:
Thomas Leonardini, Sr.

LOCATION: 2 miles south of St. Helena.

APPELLATION: Rutherford.

HOURS: 11 A.M. – 5:45 P.M. daily.

TASTINGS: $10 for current releases; price varies for reserve wines.

TOURS: None.

THE WINES: Cabernet Sauvignon, Chardonnay, dessert wine, Merlot, Sauvignon Blanc.

SPECIALTIES: Reserve Cabernet Sauvignon and Leonardini Vineyard Cabernet Sauvignon.

WINEMAKER:
Dean Sylvester.

ANNUAL PRODUCTION:
45,000 cases.

OF SPECIAL NOTE:
Chardonnay, Leonardini Vineyard Cabernet Sauvignon, and library wine selections available only at the winery.

NEARBY ATTRACTIONS:
Bothe-Napa State Park (hiking, picnicking, horseback riding, swimming Memorial Day–Labor Day; Bale Grist Mill State Historic Park (water-powered mill circa 1846); Culinary Institute of America at Greystone (cooking demonstrations); Silverado Museum (Robert Louis Stevenson memorabilia); Napa Valley Museum (winemaking displays, art exhibits).

ZD WINES

ZD WINES
8383 Silverado Trail
Napa, CA 94558
800-487-7757
info@zdwines.com
www.zdwines.com

OWNERS: deLeuze family.

LOCATION: About 2.5 miles south of Zinfandel Ln.

APPELLATION: Rutherford.

HOURS: 10 A.M.–4:30 P.M. daily.

TASTINGS: $5 for 3 or 4 current releases; $10 for 3 or 4 reserve and older vintage wines.

TOURS: By appointment.

THE WINES: Abacus (solera-style blend of ZD Reserve Cabernet Sauvignon), Cabernet Sauvignon, Chardonnay, Pinot Noir.

SPECIALTIES: Cabernet Sauvignon, Chardonnay, and Pinot Noir.

WINEMAKERS: Robert deLeuze, wine master; Chris Pisani, winemaker.

ANNUAL PRODUCTION: 30,000 cases.

OF SPECIAL NOTE: Sit-down wine and cheese seminars on Saturdays at 11 A.M. by appointment ($20, 12-person limit). Library wine tastings on Sundays at 11 A.M. by appointment ($20, 12-person limit).

NEARBY ATTRACTIONS: Bothe-Napa State Park (hiking, picnicking, horseback riding, swimming Memorial Day–Labor Day); Bale Grist Mill State Historic Park (water-powered mill circa 1846); Silverado Museum (Robert Louis Stevenson memorabilia).

Driving along the Silverado Trail through the heart of the Napa Valley, travelers are sure to notice the entrance to ZD Wines. A two-ton boulder, extracted from one of ZD's mountain vineyards, is adorned by the winery's striking gold logo, beckoning them to stop for a visit. Calla lilies intertwined with lavender welcome guests as they stroll along the path and underneath an intimate arbor to the winery entrance. The tasting room provides a cool respite on a hot summer day or a warm and cozy place to linger in front of a fireplace in the winter. Behind the tasting bar, shaped like a large barrel, are windows that allow visitors to peer into ZD's aging cellars as they sample ZD Chardonnay, Pinot Noir, and Cabernet Sauvignon.

It has been said that winemaking isn't rocket science, but in fact, founding partner Norman deLeuze had been designing liquid rocket engines for Aerojet-General in Sacramento when he met his original partner Gino Zepponi. They decided to collaborate on producing classic Pinot Noir and Chardonnay varietals and needed a name for their new enterprise. The aero-nautical industry had a quality-control program with the initials ZD, referring to Zero Defects. This matched the partners' initials and created a new association for the letters ZD. In 1969, the winery purchased Pinot Noir grapes from the Winery Lake Vineyard in Carneros in southern Sonoma and produced its first wine, the first ever labeled with the Carneros appellation. Soon after, the winery started making Chardonnay, which continues to be ZD's flagship wine.

Norman deLeuze turned to winemaking full-time, while his wife, Rosa Lee, handled sales and marketing. They purchased six acres, built their own winery, and planted Cabernet Sauvignon in Rutherford in 1979. Four years later, son Robert deLeuze was named winemaker. He had been working in ZD's cellars since he was twelve and later studied at the University of California at Davis. In 2001, Robert passed the winemaking reins to Chris Pisani, who had worked closely with Robert for five years, building his appreciation and understanding of the family's consistent winemaking style.

As ZD celebrates its thirty-fifth anniversary, it is still owned and operated by Norman, Rosa Lee, and their three adult children: Robert as wine master and CEO, Brett as president, and Julie as administrative director. Robert's two children, Brandon and Jill, began working summers and holidays at ZD in their early teens, bringing a third generation to this family affair.

SONOMA

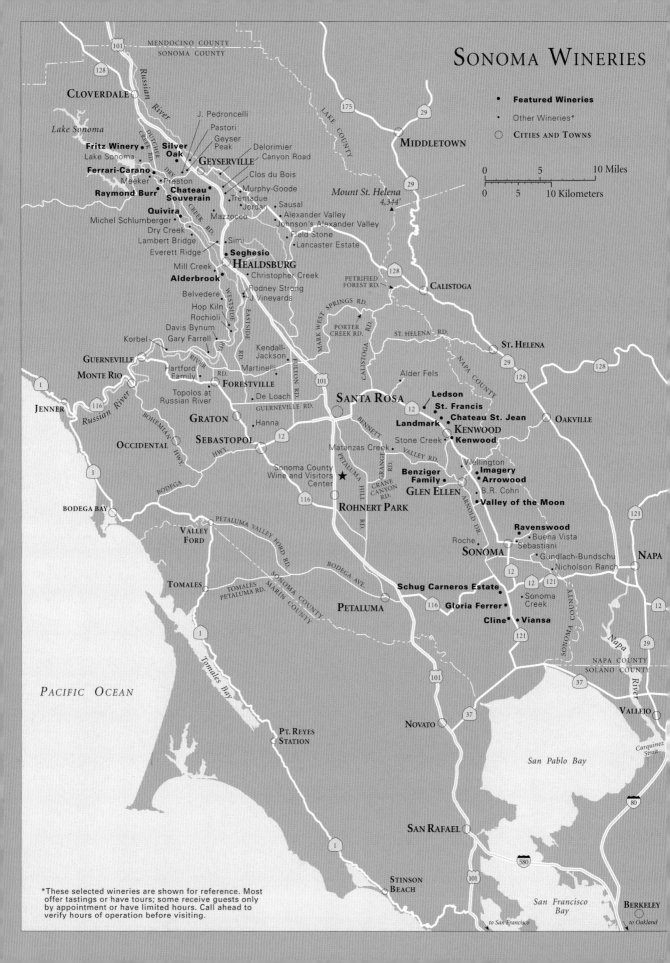

SONOMA WINERIES

- **Featured Wineries**
- Other Wineries*
- ○ CITIES AND TOWNS

*These selected wineries are shown for reference. Most offer tastings or have tours; some receive guests only by appointment or have limited hours. Call ahead to verify hours of operation before visiting.

Sonoma boasts the most geographical diversity and the highest number of appellations in wine country. From the Pacific Coast to the inland valleys, to the Mayacamas Range that defines the border with Napa County, the countryside is crisscrossed by rural roads, making it an ideal destination for casual exploration.

Some of the county's wineries can be found near the historic town of Sonoma. Facing the eight-acre central plaza are nineteenth-century adobe and false-front buildings that now house

shops, restaurants, inns, and historic sights. Diverse luminaries, such as the horticulturist Luther Burbank and the cartoonist Charles Schulz of "Peanuts" fame, made their homes in Santa Rosa; no trip would be complete without visiting the museums named for them. North and west of Santa Rosa, the Russian River wends its way to the coast, offering boating, swimming, and fishing opportunities and the shade of giant redwoods along its banks.

Healdsburg, which has quickly evolved from a quiet backwater to the hottest destination in the county, is at the hub of three major grape-growing regions—Russian River Valley, Alexander Valley, and Dry Creek Valley—all within a ten-minute drive of the town plaza.

ALDERBROOK VINEYARDS AND WINERY

Location, location, location. It's as important in the winery business as it is in residential real estate. Sun, wind, fog, drainage, altitude, exposure, soil type, and other considerations are the stuff of appellations. Some wineries, including Alderbrook Vineyards, get the best of two worlds.

The winery is situated at the southernmost tip of Dry Creek Valley and in close proximity to the Russian River Valley to the south. As a result, the Alderbrook vineyards receive the typically intense afternoon heat of Dry Creek but also some of the blessings of the ocean air that chills the Russian River Valley with the approach of evening. As the mass of air creeps up the valley from the Pacific Ocean, it produces fog in the evening and early morning. After ripening all day in the summer sunshine, the grapes are cooled down at night, giving them valuable extra time on the vines. The winery credits this extended "hang time" with providing a smooth evolution for the fruit as it develops rich, full-bodied characteristics.

When it comes to growing grapes, the right location can be a matter of mere yards. As winemaker Bryan Parker says, even vineyards located just one hundred yards apart and planted with identical vines and rootstock can produce wines with distinctly different flavors. Parker, who came to Alderbrook in 2003 from Pine Ridge Winery, spends most of his time in the vineyards trying to anticipate what they will produce, especially in regard to the winery's reserve Zinfandels. Whereas all wine grapes mature unevenly to some extent, Zinfandel is the most notorious for having clusters that contain berries in differing stages of ripeness, and Parker finds there's no substitute for personal inspection of the grapes from bud to harvest.

Sauvignon Blanc and Chardonnay are also produced from the estate vineyards. In addition to the fruit grown on its sixty-five-acre estate, the winery has agreements with top growers in both the Dry Creek Valley and the Russian River Valley appellations. Alderbrook's Pinot Noir comes from the latter, which is world renowned for this varietal.

The winery is a low-key complex of understated buildings that reminds one of the French countryside. White paint trims the edges of the balcony around the wide veranda, and an area of lush green grass beckons picnickers, who can buy delicatessen items in the spacious tasting room. The large tasting room also includes a separate "VIP" tasting room, where the winery conducts food-and-wine-pairing seminars hosted by the winemaker and the winery chef. Alderbrook prides itself on its knowledgeable staff, who further enhance guests' experience.

ALDERBROOK VINEYARDS AND WINERY
2306 Magnolia Dr.
Healdsburg, CA 95448
707-433-5987
800-405-5987
info@alderbrook.com
www.alderbrook.com

OWNER:
Terlato Wine Group.

LOCATION: Off Westside Rd. west of Healdsburg and U.S. 101.

APPELLATION:
Dry Creek Valley.

HOURS: 10 A.M.–5 P.M. daily.

TASTINGS: Complimentary.

TOURS: Contact winery for details.

THE WINES: Cabernet Sauvignon, Carignane, Chardonnay, Merlot, Pinot Noir, Sauvignon Blanc, Zinfandel.

SPECIALTIES: Dry Creek Zinfandel, Estate Chardonnay and Sauvignon Blanc, Russian River Pinot Noir.

WINEMAKER:
Bryan Parker.

ANNUAL PRODUCTION:
30,000 cases.

OF SPECIAL NOTE: Picnic items stocked in wine shop; picnicking allowed on veranda overlooking vineyards.

NEARBY ATTRACTIONS:
Russian River (swimming, canoe and kayak rentals).

ARROWOOD VINEYARDS & WINERY

ARROWOOD VINEYARDS & WINERY
14347 Hwy. 12
Glen Ellen, CA 95442
707-935-2600
hospitality@
arrowoodvineyards.com
www.arrowoodvineyards.
com

FOUNDERS: Richard and Alis Arrowood.

LOCATION: About 3 miles north of town of Sonoma via Hwy 12.

APPELLATION:
Sonoma Valley.

HOURS: 10:00 A.M.–4:30 P.M. daily.

TASTINGS: $5 for 4 wines; $10 for 4 reserve wines.

TOURS: 10:30 A.M. and 2:30 P.M. daily by appointment.

THE WINES: Cabernet Sauvignon, Chardonnay, Gewürztraminer, Malbec, Merlot, Pinot Blanc, Riesling (late harvest), Syrah, Viognier.

SPECIALTY: All wines are made from Sonoma County grapes.

WINEMAKER:
Richard Arrowood.

ANNUAL PRODUCTION:
30,000 cases.

OF SPECIAL NOTE: Extended winery and cellar tours by appointment; various events ranging from barrel-making demonstrations to food-and-wine pairings. Wine accessories, gifts, and apparel sold at winery shop.

NEARBY ATTRACTIONS:
Jack London State Historic Park (museum, hiking, horseback riding); Sonoma Valley Regional Park (hiking, dog park).

From the highway, the pair of gray, New England farmhouse–style buildings with generous porches neatly trimmed in white could easily pass for a country inn. In fact, the property was originally intended to become a bed-and-breakfast, but it never opened for business. Today, these handsome, sedate structures are home to the Arrowood Winery. The sweeping view from the wide porches encompasses the Arrowood vineyards, a neighboring winery, and the oak-studded slopes of Sonoma Mountain on the western horizon.

Richard Arrowood made his name as the longtime winemaker at Chateau St. Jean, just up the road in Kenwood. A native San Franciscan raised in Santa Rosa, he earned degrees in organic chemistry and enology, and got his start in the business in 1965 at Korbel Champagne Cellars. In 1974, the founders of Chateau St. Jean hired Arrowood as their first employee. For the next sixteen years, he made wines that earned both him and the winery worldwide attention. His reputation as one of the country's best winemakers was firmly established with his late-harvest Riesling, a varietal that he produces today under his own label.

In the late 1980s, he met and married Alis Demers, who had been working in the wine industry since 1978. Together, they began establishing the Arrowood brand. They found the perfect ten-acre property and designed their winery to blend harmoniously with the rural landscape. When they realized that they had inherited two donkeys, Burt and Ernie, from the previous landowner, they lacked the heart to kick them out and fenced off an area behind the winery.

While Richard was still at Chateau St. Jean, Alis was topping barrels or running the bottling line when she wasn't giving tours and conducting tastings. Richard began working full-time at the winery in 1990, freeing Alis to devote her energies to sales and marketing. Richard began by focusing exclusively on reserve-quality Chardonnay and Cabernet Sauvignon. Before long, he was seduced by the idea of working with less common varietals, particularly when he found exceptional fruit. Today Arrowood produces Malbec, for instance, as well as more familiar wines, all made from Sonoma County grapes. In 1998, the winery realized a long-cherished dream: opening a spacious Hospitality House next door. The building has a dramatic vaulted ceiling, an enormous stone fireplace flanked by comfortable seating, and a second-floor loft for private events. Picture windows afford magnificent views of Sonoma Valley. Visitors are welcome to walk out the huge glass doors and relax on the wraparound veranda, wineglasses in hand.

BENZIGER FAMILY WINERY

The Benziger Family Winery is laid out on a picturesque hillside of Sonoma Mountain. In this storybook setting extolled by adventure author Jack London, the Benzigers have created both an award-winning winery and a lifestyle that many would envy. Their grape-growing practices and other innovations have earned the winery kudos far and wide. The Benzigers like to share their property with visitors. The sixty-five acres of estate vineyards are accessible daily on forty-five-minute tram tours. Hauled by a tractor, the tram full of passengers is treated to a close look at the grapes, views of Sonoma Mountain, a short course in site-specific farming, a visit to spectacular wine caves, and a chance to sip a little fruit of the vine.

None of this would be possible if Mike Benziger had not followed his instincts up a narrow country road between Glen Ellen and Jack London's old Beauty Ranch. There he stumbled across a 140-year-old farmhouse—and promptly knew it was where he wanted to establish his winery. Mike's father, Bruno, was a well-established wine importer in New York, and, like most of his six siblings, Mike had worked in the family business. In 1981, Bruno helped Mike and his wife, Mary, purchase the property, which was to become the original Glen Ellen Winery. In short order, the elder Benzigers followed their son, as did Mike's six siblings.

Throughout the 1980s, the Benzigers enjoyed great success building the Glen Ellen brand. In 1993, the family shifted its focus to ultrapremium wines. They sold the Glen Ellen label—but not the vineyards or the winery—and established the Benziger Family Winery on the same site. The winery currently uses three hundred lots of grapes from more than sixty ranches in more than a dozen appellations. At their property and in concert with outside growers, the Benzigers practice extensive site-specific farming techniques such as canopy manipulation to maximize desirable flavors. For example, if a Cabernet Sauvignon vineyard consistently produces the green olive flavors associated with cool temperatures and low light, increasing the vine's exposure to sunlight by reducing the canopy would result in more heat and more desirable blackberry, chocolate, or minty flavors. The estate is now biodynamically farmed. These small but steady innovations have proven successful in maximizing the potential flavor intensity for each vineyard. The Benziger family story may not be Jack London material, but you can't beat it for a happy ending.

BENZIGER FAMILY WINERY
1883 London Ranch Rd.
Glen Ellen, CA 95442
888-490-2739
greatwine@benziger.com
www.benziger.com

OWNERS: Benziger family.

LOCATION: 1 mile west of Glen Ellen via London Ranch Rd.

APPELLATION: Sonoma Mountain.

HOURS: 10 A.M.–5 P.M. daily.

TASTINGS: $5 for 5 wines; $10 for 5 wines in Private Estate Wine Room.

TOURS: Vineyard Tram Tours ($10) includes tasting and self-guided tours.

THE WINES: Cabernet Sauvignon, Chardonnay, Fumé Blanc, Merlot, Muscat Canelli, Pinot Noir, Sauvignon Blanc, Syrah, Zinfandel.

SPECIALTIES: Tribute (Cabernet Sauvignon blend) and vineyard-designated and reserve wines.

WINEMAKER: Terry Nolan.

ANNUAL PRODUCTION: 150,000 cases.

OF SPECIAL NOTE: Estate and limited-production wines available only at winery. Children's play area; peacock aviary; wine caves; display of antique farm and winery equipment. Wine accessories, home furnishings, and cookbooks sold at winery shop.

NEARBY ATTRACTIONS: Jack London State Historic Park (museum, hiking, horseback riding); Sonoma Valley Regional Park (hiking, dog park); Morton's Sonoma Springs Resort (swimming, picnicking).

Chateau Souverain Winery

Chateau Souverain Winery
400 Souverain Rd.
Geyserville, CA 95441
888-80-WINES
www.chateausouverain.com

Owner: Beringer Blass
Wine Estates.

Location: About 5 miles
north of Healdsburg via
U.S. 101.

Appellation:
Alexander Valley.

Hours: 10 a.m.–5 p.m. daily.

Tastings: $5 (applied to
wine purchase).

Tours: None.

The Wines: Cabernet
Sauvignon, Chardonnay,
Merlot, Sauvignon Blanc,
Syrah, Zinfandel.

Specialties: Cabernet
Sauvignon, Chardonnay.

Winemaker: Ed Killian.

Annual Production:
145,000 cases.

Of Special Note: Chateau
Souverain Library Reserve
Cabernet Sauvignon,
Mourvedre, Syrah Port,
Viognier, and Reserve
Zinfandel available only at
winery. Bottle limits on
some small-production
wines and reserve wines.
Food and wine accessories,
apparel, glassware, and
books sold in winery
shop. Two picnic areas;
restaurant open for lunch
daily and for dinner
Friday–Sunday.

Nearby Attractions:
Lake Sonoma (boating,
camping, hiking).

The imposing chateau perched on a knoll makes this winery one of the most impressive sights in Sonoma County. Approaching the estate beneath an arch connecting two tall stone pillars, visitors often feel a sense of occasion. The driveway, lined with gray-green olive trees, is surrounded by Cabernet Sauvignon vines whose colors and textures change with the season, from bleak and gnarled in the dead of winter to a lush green canopy in spring and summer, to a palette of gold and orange as harvest approaches in the fall.

The twenty-five-acre grounds are a mixture of casual landscaping, including some 180 rose-bushes, and the kind of formal gardens that befit a chateau. The buildings appear to consist almost entirely of steeply pitched slate-tile roofs, an impression that heightens the dramatic effect. A broad staircase leads from the parking lot to a gravel-lined courtyard where wooden benches face a square pool with a fountain in the middle. Around the courtyard are small trees, roses, and lavender plants. Flowering vines climb the walls of the winery. The ambience is undeniably Mediterranean.

Chateau Souverain Winery was designed by architect John Marsh Davis and built in 1973. Blending the feel of a French chateau with elements of the historic Sonoma hop kilns that once proliferated in this part of the county, Davis constructed two prominent towers connected by a long, low-rise building that houses the wine cellar. One tower serves as the business offices. The other, the one guests see when they approach the winery, is home to the tasting room as well as the winery's restaurant, the Alexander Valley Grille. Davis's design won an American Institute of Architects Design Excellence Award in 1974.

The expansive views from Chateau Souverain's courtyard and the tasting room encompass the estate vineyards in the foreground and the profile of 4,344-foot Mount St. Helena to the east. The most spectacular vistas are available from the outdoor tables at the winery's restaurant. This bistro-style establishment specializes in regional fare such as fresh seafood, artisanal cheeses, free-range poultry, and seasonal organic produce. Chef Martin Courtman, who has been at the winery since 1991, honors local purveyors by listing their names on the back of the menu. Courtman has instituted a daily afternoon Al Fresco Menu that lists a three-tiered stand of small bites and flights of wine to match. The wines offered to restaurant patrons are from Chateau Souverain, which showcases the best grapes from the winery's estate vineyards, as well as from the top Sonoma County viticultural areas for each variety.

CHATEAU ST. JEAN WINERY

With the dramatic profile of Sugarloaf Ridge as a backdrop, the exquisitely landscaped grounds at Chateau St. Jean in Kenwood evoke the image of a grand country estate. The chateau itself dates to the 1920s, but it wasn't until 1973 that a family of Central Valley, California, growers of table grapes founded the winery. They named it after a favorite relative and, with tongue in cheek, placed a statue of "St. Jean" in the garden.

The winery building was constructed from the ground up to suit Chateau St. Jean's particular style of winemaking. The founders believed in the European practice of creating vineyard-designated wines, so they designed the winery to accommodate numerous lots of grapes, which could be kept separate throughout the winemaking process. Wines from each special vineyard are also bottled and marketed separately, with the vineyard name on the label. The winery produces eleven vineyard-designated wines from the Sonoma Valley, Alexander Valley, Russian River Valley, and Carneros appellations. The winery also makes other premium varietals and one famously successful blend.

Chateau St. Jean became the first Sonoma winery to be awarded the prestigious Wine of the Year award from *Wine Spectator* magazine for its 1996 Cinq Cépages, a Bordeaux-style blend of five varieties. The winery received high aclaim again when it was given the #2 Wine of the Year from *Wine Spectator* for its 1999 Cinq Cépages Cabernet Sauvignon. Winemaker Margo Van Staaveren has more than twenty years of vineyard and winemaking experience with Chateau St. Jean, and her knowledge of Sonoma further underscores her excellence in highlighting the best of each vineyard.

In the summer of 2000, Chateau St. Jean opened the doors to its new Visitor Center and Gardens. A formal Mediterranean-style garden contains roses, herbs, and citrus trees planted in oversized terra-cotta urns arranged to create a number of open-air "rooms." Picnickers have always been welcome to relax on the winery's redwood-studded grounds, but now the setting is enhanced by the extensive plantings, making the one-acre garden attractive throughout the year. Beyond the Mediterranean garden is the tasting room with a custom-made tasting bar. Fashioned from mahogany with ebony accents, the thirty-five-foot-long bar is topped with sheet zinc. The elegant chateau houses the Reserve Tasting Room. Visitors who would like to learn more about Chateau St. Jean wines are encouraged to attend the winery's various educational seminars. Introductory classes are offered daily, while more in-depth programs are available by reservation.

CHATEAU ST. JEAN WINERY
8555 Hwy. 12
Kenwood, CA 95452
707-833-4134
www.chateaustjean.com

OWNER: Beringer Blass Wine Estates.

LOCATION: 8 miles east of Santa Rosa off U.S. 101.

APPELLATION: Sonoma Valley.

HOURS: 10 A.M.–5 P.M. daily.

TASTINGS: $5 for 3 wines in Tasting Room; $10 in Reserve Tasting Room.

TOURS: By appointment.

THE WINES: Cabernet Franc, Cabernet Sauvignon, Chardonnay, Fumé Blanc, Gewürztraminer, Johannisberg Riesling, Late-Harvest Johannisberg Riesling, Merlot, Pinot Blanc, Pinot Noir, Viognier.

SPECIALTIES: Single vineyard–designated wines.

WINEMAKER: Margo Van Staaveren.

ANNUAL PRODUCTION: 300,000 cases.

OF SPECIAL NOTE: Picnic tables in oak-and-redwood grove. Classes and seminars on wine. Open houses on most holidays. Large store offering local cheeses, meats, and breads, as well as other merchandise.

NEARBY ATTRACTIONS: Sugarloaf Ridge State Park (hiking, camping, horseback riding).

CLINE CELLARS

CLINE CELLARS
24737 Hwy. 121
Sonoma, CA 95476
707-940-4000
800-546-2070
info@clinecellars.com
www.clinecellars.com

OWNERS:
Fred and Nancy Cline.

LOCATION: About 5 miles
south of the town of
Sonoma.

APPELLATION: Carneros.

HOURS: 10 A.M.–6 P.M. daily.

TASTINGS: Complimentary.

TOURS: 11 A.M., 1 P.M., and
3 P.M. daily.

THE WINES: Carignane,
Marsanne, Mourvèdre,
Pinot Gris, Syrah,
Viognier, Zinfandel.

SPECIALTIES: Zinfandel and
Rhône-style wines.

WINEMAKER:
Charles Tsegeletos.

ANNUAL PRODUCTION:
200,000 cases.

OF SPECIAL NOTE: Turtles
and fish in mineral pools
built in the 1880s for
raising carp. 130-year-old
graffiti on old bathhouse
wall. Cookbooks, deli
items, and condiments
sold in winery shop.

NEARBY ATTRACTIONS:
Vintage Aircraft (scenic
and aerobatic biplane
rides); Infineon Raceway
(auto racing); Train Town
(rides for children).

Five thousand rosebushes stand shoulder to shoulder beside the low stone wall that winds its way onto the winery grounds. From April through December, they provide a riot of fragrant pink, white, red, and yellow blossoms. Picnic tables are scattered around the lawn, shaded by magnolias and other trees. Weeping willows hover over the mineral pools on either side of the restored 1850s farmhouse where the tasting room is located. The white farmhouse is rimmed with a picturesque dark green porch set with small wrought-iron tables and chairs where visitors can sip wine at their leisure.

Cline Cellars was originally established in Oakley, California, some forty miles east of San Francisco. Founder Fred Cline had spent his childhood summers learning farming and winemaking from his grandfather, Valeriano Jacuzzi (of spa and pump fame). Cline started the winery in 1982 with a $12,000 inheritance from the sale of Jacuzzi Bros. Four years later, his brother Matt joined Cline Cellars as the winemaker after studying viticulture at the University of California at Davis. In 1991, the Cline Cellars facilities were relocated to this 350-acre estate in the Carneros District at the southern end of the Sonoma Valley.

The Cline estate occupies a historical parcel of land first settled by the Miwok Indians. Nearby, a nineteenth-century bathhouse harks to the time when the white settlers realized something that the Miwoks had known all along: warm mineral baths are good for you. While the town of Sonoma is generally considered the original site of the Sonoma mission, the mission was actually founded here when Father Altimira installed a cross on July 4, 1823. Perhaps it was the constant Carneros breezes that inspired him to pull up stakes and relocate to the town of Sonoma later that same year.

The Clines specialize in Zinfandel and Rhône varietals. Their Ancient Vines Carignane, Zinfandel, and Mourvèdre wines are produced from some of the oldest and rarest vines in the state. The Mourvèdre grapevines represent approximately 85 percent of California's total supply of this versatile varietal. The Sonoma location was selected especially for its relatively cool climate; chilly fog and frequent strong afternoon winds mitigate the summertime heat that blisters the rest of the Sonoma Valley. When the Clines bought the property, they planted all-new vineyards of Rhône varietals such as Syrah, Viognier, Marsanne, and Roussanne.

FERRARI-CARANO VINEYARDS AND WINERY

Ferrari-Carano is well known for its critically acclaimed wines, but to some people, the winery is even more famous for its gardens, five acres that explode with color from the thousands of tulips in early spring through the last blush of 200 rose bushes in late fall. Visitors enter through wrought-iron gates that lead to meandering pathways set beside a rippling stream, which is guided into two waterfalls that flow into sparkling ponds filled with fish. The gardens are Italian-French parterre in style, but that formality is offset with texture and color from perennial and annual flowers and an array of trees and shrubs.

Rhonda Carano began designing the landscaping in 1992, when the winery broke ground on its hospitality center, Villa Fiore (House of Flowers), which opened five years later. By then, Don and Rhonda Carano had been making wine for nearly two decades. Both second-generation Italian-Americans, the Caranos visited Sonoma County in the late 1970s and were immediately taken with the area's natural beauty and its dramatic resemblance to Italy. The high quality of the local wines sealed the deal.  In short order, they bought a sixty-acre parcel in the Alexander Valley with thirty acres of grapes. The Caranos studied winemaking at the University of California at Davis and began seeking more vineyard acquisitions. In 1981, with the purchase of a vineyard property in nearby Dry Creek Valley, they embarked on building their dream, Ferrari-Carano Vineyards and Winery.

Winemaker George Bursick came to work for the Caranos in 1985. That year, as construction on the Dry Creek Valley property began, they made the first Ferrari-Carano wine—2,500 cases of Chardonnay, all of which sold out—in the barn in Alexander Valley. Today, Ferrari-Carano obtains grapes from eighteen vineyards in four appellations: Dry Creek Valley, Alexander Valley, and Russian River Valley in Sonoma and Carneros in Napa. Owning more than 2,500 acres of land in Sonoma, including 1,200 acres planted to wine grapes, gives the Caranos complete control over vineyard practices and grape selection.

When the winemaking facility in Dry Creek Valley was completed, the Caranos broke ground on Villa Fiore. The 25,000-square-foot Italianate-style structure has dramatic stone arches and columns, sienna-colored stucco walls, and a red-tile roof. Inside the villa's tasting room, visitors find a honey-colored coffered ceiling of hand-tooled bird's-eye maple, a mahogany and black granite tasting bar, and marbleized walls and flooring. They also find an outstanding marketplace specializing in tabletop items that reflect the Caranos' passion for wine, food, and hospitality—Italian style.

FERRARI-CARANO VINEYARDS AND WINERY
8761 Dry Creek Rd.
Healdsburg, CA 95448
707-433-6700
800-831-0381
customerservice@fcwinery.com
tourinformation@ferrari-carano.com
www.ferrari-carano.com

OWNERS:
Don and Rhonda Carano.

LOCATION: About 9 miles west of Hwy. 101 via Dry Creek Rd.

APPELLATION:
Dry Creek Valley.

HOURS: 10 A.M.–5 P.M. daily.

TASTINGS: $3 for 4 current releases (applicable to purchase).

TOURS: 10 A.M. Monday–Saturday, by appointment.

THE WINES: Cabernet Sauvignon, Chardonnay, Fumé Blanc, Merlot, Syrah, Zinfandel.

SPECIALTIES: Mountain-grown red wines and Sangiovese.

WINEMAKER:
George Bursick.

ANNUAL PRODUCTION:
150,000 cases.

OF SPECIAL NOTE: Villa Fiore label wines available only at winery. Gift shop featuring tableware, linens, gourmet foods, and Sonoma County products. Local events include Taste of Spring (spring) and Holiday Affair (November).

NEARBY ATTRACTIONS:
Lake Sonoma (boating, camping, hiking).

FRITZ WINERY

FRITZ WINERY
24691 Dutcher Creek Rd.
Cloverdale, CA 95425
707-894-3389
800-418-9463
info@fritzwinery.com
www.fritzwinery.com

PRESIDENT:
Clayton B. Fritz.

LOCATION: About 1 mile southwest of intersection of U.S. 101 and Dutcher Creek Rd.

APPELLATION:
Dry Creek Valley.

HOURS: 10:30 A.M.–4:30 P.M. daily.

TASTINGS: Complimentary for all wines.

TOURS: By appointment.

THE WINES: Cabernet Sauvignon, Carignane, Chardonnay, Late-Harvest Zinfandel, Old Vine Zinfandel, Pinot Noir, Rockpile Cabernet Sauvignon, Sauvignon Blanc, Zinfandel.

SPECIALTIES: Chardonnay, Pinot Noir, Zinfandel.

WINEMAKER:
Christina Pallmann.

ANNUAL PRODUCTION:
18,000 cases.

OF SPECIAL NOTE: Rogers' Reserve Zinfandel, Late-Harvest Zinfandel, Ruxton Chardonnay, and Carignane available only at winery. Annual events include Winter Wineland (January), Barrel Tasting (March), and Dry Creek Passport Weekend (April).

NEARBY ATTRACTIONS:
Russian River (swimming, canoe and kayak rentals); Lake Sonoma (boating, camping, hiking).

What began as an idyllic family retreat is now a thriving family business on the northern edge of the Dry Creek Valley. Jay and Barbara Fritz were seeking an escape from the summertime fog and bustle of San Francisco when they found this rugged, hundred-plus-acre property on a remote hillside back in 1970. They dammed a spring to create "Lake Fritz" and created a home away from home. Son Clayton Fritz spent his childhood summers there, although it has been a long time since he swam in the pond. Now, as president of the winery built in 1979—still the northernmost facility in Sonoma County—and as the only one of the three siblings to work there, he is far too busy looking after day-to-day operations.

Construction of the winery began when energy crises were commonplace. The idea of an energy-efficient, subterranean winery seemed logical, especially given the capacity to create a gravity-flow production system.

The unique three-tier structure allows crushing to be done on top of the winery, and from there the juice is sent underground to the top floor. When the time is ripe, small lots of wine are sent, via one-inch hoses, a level deeper. White wines are aged in a barrel room underground; red wines mature in the adjoining cave. This system eliminates the need for pumping equipment; refrigeration is required only to cool the fermentation tanks.

The winery farms Sauvignon Blanc, Zinfandel, and Cabernet Sauvignon vineyards in the hot, arid Dry Creek Valley. Increasingly, Fritz buys Pinot Noir and Chardonnay grapes from the nearby Russian River Valley, where the cool climate regulates the ripening of the grapes, a portion of them from Dutton Ranch, known for producing some of the finest fruit in the Russian River area. Fritz Winery instituted some drastic changes in 1996, slashing annual production to twelve thousand cases from nearly thirty thousand. The figure has increased since to almost eighteen thousand. The winery is beginning to harvest some of the twenty acres of Pinot Noir acquired in the Russian River Valley in the late 1990s. When that vineyard is in full production, probably around 2005, production will probably top out at twenty-one thousand cases. As the winery works toward this goal, the winemaker, Christina Pallmann, will have input from one of the industry's most highly regarded consultants, Merry Edwards.

Visitors who troop up the hill can enjoy a view of Lake Fritz from the patio, where white market umbrellas provide shade for round tables just outside the tasting room. Rockroses and other hardy plants give way to wild grasses as the hill slopes down to the water's edge.

GLORIA FERRER CHAMPAGNE CAVES

The Carneros District, with its continual winds and cool marine air, is known far and wide as an ideal climate for growing Pinot Noir and Chardonnay grapes. The word spread all the way to Spain, where the Ferrer family had been making sparkling wine for more than a century. In 1889, Pedro Ferrer founded Freixenet, now one of the world's two largest producers of sparkling wine.

Members of the family had been looking for vineyard land in the United States off and on for fifty years when José and Gloria Ferrer visited the southern part of the Sonoma Valley. The climate reminded them of their Catalan home in Spain, and in 1982, they acquired a forty-acre pasture and then, four years later, another two hundred acres nearby. They started planting vineyards with Pinot Noir and Chardonnay, the traditional sparkling wine grapes. In addition to sparkling wines, Gloria Ferrer produces still wines, including Merlot, Pinot Noir, and Chardonnay.

The wines have a history of critical success. Within a year of its 1986 debut, the winery won seven gold medals and a Sweepstakes Award at the San Francisco Fair's International Wine Competition.

The winery that José Ferrer built was the first champagne facility in the Carneros. Named for his wife, it was designed after a *masia* (a Catalan farmhouse), complete with terraces, a red tile roof, and thick walls the color of the Spanish plains. Complementing the exterior, the winery's cool interior has dark tile floors and Spanish textiles. The ties to Spain continue in the winery's shop, which offers a selection of cookbooks devoted to Spanish cuisine and the specialties of Catalonia. Also available are several Sonoma-grown products such as Gloria Ferrer's champagne-filled chocolates, mustards and dipping sauces, and a selection of table condiments.

Visitors are welcome to enjoy Gloria Ferrer wines, both still and sparkling, in the spacious tasting room—where a fire roars in the fireplace on winter days—or outside on the Vista Terrace. There they are treated to a breathtaking view of the Carneros District and the upper reaches of San Pablo Bay. On a clear day, they can see all the way to the peak of 3,848-foot Mount Diablo in the East Bay. Both still and sparkling wines are aged in the caves tunneled into the hill behind the hospitality center. Winery tours include a visit to these aromatic dark recesses where guides explain the traditional *méthode champenoise* process of creating sparkling wine, during which the wine undergoes its secondary fermentation—the one that forms the characteristic bubbles— in the bottle, not in the barrel.

GLORIA FERRER CHAMPAGNE CAVES
23555 Hwy. 121
Sonoma, CA 95476
707-996-7256
info@gloriaferrer.com
www.gloriaferrer.com

OWNER: Freixenet, S.A.

LOCATION: 6 miles south of town of Sonoma.

APPELLATION: Carneros.

HOURS: 10:30 A.M.–5:30 P.M. daily.

TASTINGS: $4–10 per glass of sparkling wine; $1–3 for table wine.

TOURS: Daily during hours of operation.

THE WINES: Blanc de Noirs, Brut, Brut Rosé, Chardonnay, Merlot, Pinot Noir, Syrah.

SPECIALTIES: Brut Rosé, José S. Ferrer Reserve, Carneros Cuvée, Gravel Knob Vineyard Pinot Noir, Rust Rock Terrace Pinot Noir.

WINEMAKER: Bob Iantosca.

ANNUAL PRODUCTION: 100,000 cases.

OF SPECIAL NOTE: Spanish cookbooks and locally made products, as well as deli items, sold at the winery. Annual Catalan Festival (July).

NEARBY ATTRACTIONS: Mission San Francisco Solano and other historic buildings in downtown Sonoma; Vintage Aircraft (scenic and aerobatic biplane rides); Infineon Raceway (auto racing); Viansa Winery Wetlands (tours).

IMAGERY ESTATE WINERY

IMAGERY ESTATE WINERY
14335 Hwy. 12
Glen Ellen, CA 95442
707-935-4515
877-550-4278
info@imagerywinery.com
www.imagerywinery.com

OWNERS: Benziger family.

LOCATION: 3 miles north of the town of Sonoma via Hwy. 12.

APPELLATION: Sonoma Valley.

HOURS: 10 A.M.–4:30 P.M. daily.

TASTINGS: $5 for 5 wines.

TOURS: Weekends by appointment.

THE WINES: Barbera, Cabernet Franc, Cabernet Sauvignon, Chardonnay, Lagrein, Malbec, Petite Sirah, Pinot Blanc, Port, Sangiovese, Viognier, White Burgundy.

SPECIALTIES: Limited-production varietals.

WINEMAKER: Joe Benziger.

ANNUAL PRODUCTION: 5,000 cases.

OF SPECIAL NOTE: Most wines available only in tasting room. Gallery of 175 original artworks commissioned by winery; patio seating; picnic area; bocce ball court. Limited-edition wine-label posters and extensive collection of serving pieces at winery shop.

NEARBY ATTRACTIONS: Jack London State Historic Park (museum, hiking, horseback riding); Sonoma Valley Regional Park (hiking, dog park).

When is a wine bottle more than just a wine bottle? When it is adorned with an original work of art. This is the case for the wines in the Imagery Estate Winery's Artist Collection, each bottle of which has a distinctive label bearing artwork. The contemporary artists commissioned to create the labels include Robert Arneson, Chester Arnold, Squeak Carnwath, Roy De Forest, Mary Frank, David Gilhooly, David Nash, Nathan Oliveira, William Wiley, and Chihung Yang. The winery itself is almost as much a gallery as it is a winemaking facility and even has its own curator, Bob Nugent, a recognized artist with strong ties to the national art community. Nugent has organized the 175 pieces of original label art into a permanent display in the hospitality center. Like the winemaking facility behind it, the hospitality center is in an earth-toned modern building that is surprisingly compatible with the bucolic Sonoma Valley.

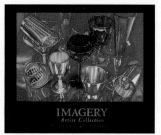

The most important artist at the winery, however, is Joe Benziger. A member of the acclaimed family that runs the nearby Benziger Family Winery, Joe Benziger has been the creative force behind the Imagery wines since their inception. He handles every detail of the winery's two tiers, the Artist Collection and the Vineyard Collection. The Artist Collection is known for its limited quantities of uncommon varietal offerings, such as Petite Sirah and Malbec. The newer Vineyard Collection features only select, single-vineyard wines from exceptional vineyards throughout Sonoma, Napa, and North Coast appellations.

The original Artist Collection dates to 1985, when the owners of Benziger Family Winery and Imagery Estate Winery found themselves with two small lots of exceptional Chardonnay and Zinfandel. The challenge was to find a way to showcase wines that were too limited to market nationally but too special to ignore. As serendipity would have it, winemaker Joe Benziger happened to meet Bob Nugent at a local polo match. That encounter led to Nugent's creation of a wine label. By the second vintage, the concept evolved as a way to focus on esoteric grape varietals not readily available in most winery offerings.

The Imagery Estate wines became so popular that in the summer of 2000, the family moved the entire operation, including the winemaking facilities and the artwork, to their property on Highway 12, less than two miles from the Benziger Family Winery. This is where visitors now come to taste the wines and linger to admire the art collection, the largest of its kind in the United States.

KENWOOD VINEYARDS

The photogenic, century-old barn where visitors come to taste Kenwood's wines dates to one of the most romantic eras in Sonoma Valley history. The quintessential adventure author Jack London was living, writing, and raising grapes in nearby Glen Ellen when the Pagani Brothers established their winery in 1906 in the buildings that now house Kenwood Vineyards. In those days, long before the invention of tasting rooms, wine lovers would bring their own barrels and jugs to be filled and then cart them home.

Decades later, in 1970, a trio of wine enthusiasts from the San Francisco Bay Area founded Kenwood Vineyards. In redesigning and modernizing the existing winery, they created a facility that allows the winemaker the utmost in flexibility. More than 125 stainless steel fermenting and upright oak tanks are utilized in combination with some 17,000 French and American oak barrels. Kenwood uses estate fruit as well as grapes from some of Sonoma County's best vineyards and follows the *cuvée* winemaking method, in which the harvest from each vineyard is handled separately to preserve its individual character. According to winemaker Michael Lee, one of the winery's founders, such "small lot" winemaking allows each lot of grapes to be brought to its fullest potential before blending. Likewise, the acclaimed Artist Series is a masterful blend of the top barrels of Cabernet Sauvignon.

The historic barn and other original buildings lend a nostalgic ambience to the modern winemaking facilities on the twenty-two-acre estate. But there is another link to the romantic history of the Valley of the Moon, as author London dubbed Sonoma Valley.

Best known for his rugged individualism and dynamic writing, London was also an accomplished farmer and rancher. At the heart of his Beauty Ranch—now part of the Jack London State Historic Park—several hundred acres of vineyards were planted in the 1870s on terraced slopes. The volcanic ash fields produced excellent wines by the turn of the twentieth century. London died in 1916, and by World War II, his crop fields had become overgrown. But in 1976, Kenwood Vineyards became the exclusive marketer of wines produced from the ranch. The Cabernet Sauvignon, Zinfandel, Merlot, and Pinot Noir, made only from Jack London vineyard grapes, bear a label with the image of a wolf's head, London's signature stamp.

Known for consistency of quality in both its red and its white wines, Kenwood produces mostly moderately priced wines. The major exception is the Artist Series Cabernet Sauvignons, which have been collector's items since first released in 1978.

KENWOOD VINEYARDS
9592 Hwy. 12
Kenwood, CA 95452
707-833-5891
info@heckestates.com
www.kenwoodvineyards.com

OWNER: F. Korbel & Bros.

LOCATION: 15 miles southeast of Santa Rosa on Hwy. 12.

APPELLATION: Sonoma Valley.

HOURS: 10 A.M.–4:30 P.M. daily.

TASTINGS: Complimentary; $5 for Private Reserve wines.

TOURS: None.

THE WINES: Cabernet Sauvignon, Chardonnay, Gewürztraminer, Merlot, Pinot Noir, Sauvignon Blanc, sparkling wines, White Zinfandel, Zinfandel.

SPECIALTIES: Artist Series, Jack London Ranch wines.

WINEMAKER: Pat Henderson.

ANNUAL PRODUCTION: 550,000 cases.

OF SPECIAL NOTE: Monthly themed food-and-wine events matching chef's specialties with appropriate wines. Limited-release Artist Series wines available only at winery.

NEARBY ATTRACTIONS: Jack London State Historic Park (museum, hiking, horseback riding); Sugarloaf Ridge State Park (hiking, camping, horseback riding).

LANDMARK VINEYARDS

LANDMARK VINEYARDS
101 Adobe Canyon Rd.
Kenwood, CA 95452
707-833-0053
info@landmarkwine.com
www.landmarkwine.com

OWNERS: Mary and Michael Colhoun.

LOCATION: 11.5 miles north of town of Sonoma off Hwy. 12.

APPELLATION: Sonoma Valley.

HOURS: 10 A.M.–4:30 P.M. daily.

TASTINGS: Complimentary.

TOURS: By appointment.

THE WINES: Chardonnay, Pinot Noir, Syrah.

SPECIALTY: Handcrafted wines fermented with wild yeast.

WINEMAKER: Eric Stern.

ANNUAL PRODUCTION: 25,000 cases.

OF SPECIAL NOTE: Pondside picnic area; bocce ball court; horse-drawn wagon rides in vineyards (summer weekends only). Range of picnic baskets and wine-related accessories at winery shop.

NEARBY ATTRACTIONS: Sugarloaf State Park (hiking, camping, horseback riding); Annadel State Park (hiking, biking).

The low-rise California mission–style architecture of Landmark Vineyards looks so appropriate to the site that the buildings might have been there for a century. This family-owned winery was actually built in 1987, when founder Damaris Deere Ethridge decided to relocate her winery in northwestern Sonoma County to this twenty-acre estate in the heart of Sonoma Valley. The elegant complex surrounded by vineyards is graced with abundant natural light and expansive views of the forested slopes of Sugarloaf Mountain. A brick walkway lined with rosebushes leads from the entrance into a courtyard showcasing a low blue-tiled fountain that sends a spray of water nearly twenty feet. Around the fountain are six Italian cypress, planted in a semicircle.

One element that might seem curious to first-time visitors is the bright green, 1946 John Deere tractor displayed near the entrance to the winery. But this is a very fitting artifact, since founder Damaris Ethridge is a direct descendant of John Deere, who invented the steel plow in 1838 and thus changed the American agricultural landscape forever. The family's commitment to innovation and respect for the land remains evident today in its approach to winemaking.

Michael Deere Colhoun, who owns Landmark Vineyards with his wife, Mary T. Colhoun, is credited with the vision and talent that transformed what was once a little-known winery into one of the most heralded producers of Chardonnay, Pinot Noir, and Syrah in California. While many wineries make a wide range of wines, Landmark decided to specialize in just three. Key to the winery's success is the careful selection of vineyards, each of which is chosen for the ability of its grapes to produce stellar wine.

Equally important is the use of wild yeasts contained in the waxy coating, or bloom, of the grape skin, as well as yeasts that occur naturally in the local environment, in place of factory-produced yeasts. When the grape juice is transferred into French oak barrels, the wild yeasts not only transform the juice into wine, but also create a wide array of secondary compounds that lend the wines great depth and complexity. The incorporation of these naturally occurring yeasts is integral to the traditional Burgundian style of winemaking.

The centerpiece of the Landmark tasting room is a dramatic mural painted on canvas by noted Sonoma County artist Claudia Wagar. Hovering between impressionism and realism, the imagery unfolds from foreground to background—from a close-up of a grape cluster against grapevines in neat rows to the rolling green hills of Sonoma Valley and Sugarloaf Mountain in the background.

LEDSON WINERY AND VINEYARDS

Locals call it "the castle"—the Gothic edifice that took ten years and some 2 million bricks to create. As they drove up and down the highway in front of it, they wondered if it was a house or an elegant winery. When the Ledson family started construction in 1989, they thought the property would be ideal for their residence. They planted Merlot and Zinfandel vineyards and began work on the house. As the months passed, the turrets, slate roofs, balconies, and fountains took shape, and passersby would even climb over the fences to get a better look.

Steve Ledson finally realized it was time to rethink his plan. Given the intense public interest in the building and the quality of his grape harvests—which he sold to nearby wineries—he decided to turn the sixteen-thousand-square-foot structure into a winery and tasting room. In 1997, he released the winery's first wine: the 1994 Estate Merlot. After two years of reconstruction, the winery opened in 1999.

Fortunately, Ledson not only had his own construction company but also benefited from his family's history of farming in the area, beginning in the 1860s. His grandmother's father was an early pioneer in Sonoma County winemaking, and both sets of grandparents had worked their adjoining Sonoma Valley ranches cooperatively. Eventually, this Ledson acreage became part of Annadel State Park. Steve Ledson, the fourth generation to farm in the area, had always wanted to grow grapes, and when he had the chance, he bought the twenty-one-acre property—which just happened to have a view of Annadel park.

Visitors to the castle today find an estate worthy of the French countryside, with a grand brick driveway, a manicured landscape, and a flourishing collection of roses. Just inside the front door is a huge curved staircase and three spacious rooms for tasting and shopping. The curious will delight in finding remnants of the original architecture, such as mini-Gothic fireplaces in the retail shop. The interior was designed entirely by Steve Ledson and features ornate wood inlays and mosaics created by son Mike.

The Marketplace at Ledson proffers an impressive selection of international gourmet products, including more than a hundred cheeses from around the world and premium meats, as well as imported and local olive oils. Also featured are freshly baked breads, homemade salads, fresh local produce, and sandwiches. Guests are encouraged to create their own wine country picnic for enjoying in the century-old oak grove next to the vineyard or alongside the fountain. Then, they have only to cross the street to hike the miles of trails in Annadel State Park.

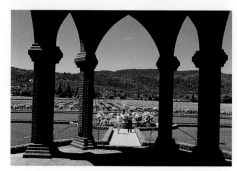

LEDSON WINERY AND VINEYARDS
7335 Hwy. 12
Kenwood, CA 95409
707-537-3810
www.ledson.com

OWNER:
Steve Noble Ledson.

LOCATION: About 2 mi. northwest of Kenwood.

APPELLATION:
Sonoma Valley.

HOURS: 10 A.M.–5 P.M. daily.

TASTINGS: $5 for 5 wines; $10 for 5 reserve and library wines.

TOURS: None.

THE WINES: Barbera, Cabernet Sauvignon, Chardonnay, Dolcetto, Gewürztraminer, Johannisberg Riesling, Merlot, Orange Muscat, Pinot Grigio, Pinot Noir, Port, Sangiovese, Sauvignon Blanc, Syrah, Zinfandel.

SPECIALTY: Small lots of handcrafted Merlot, Chardonnay, Cabrnet Sauvignon, and Zinfandel.

WINEMAKER:
Steve Noble Ledson.

ANNUAL PRODUCTION: 28,000 cases.

OF SPECIAL NOTE: Ledson wines available only at winery and at fine restaurants. Six-room Ledson Hotel & Harmony Club, in the town of Sonoma on Sonoma Plaza, includes a wine bar and has the same distinctive charm as the winery.

NEARBY ATTRACTIONS: Sugarloaf State Park (hiking, camping, horseback riding); Annadel State Park (hiking, biking).

QUIVIRA ESTATE VINEYARDS & WINERY

QUIVIRA ESTATE VINEYARDS & WINERY
4900 West Dry Creek Rd.
Healdsburg, CA 95448
800-292-8339
quivira@quivirawine.com
www.quivirawine.com

OWNERS: Henry and
Holly Wendt.

LOCATION: 5 miles
northwest of Healdsburg
via Dry Creek Rd. and
Lambert Bridge Rd.

APPELLATION:
Dry Creek Valley.

HOURS: 11 A.M.–5 P.M. daily.
Call for holiday hours.

TASTINGS: Complimentary.

TOURS: Weekdays, by
appointment.

THE WINES: Petite Sirah,
Sauvignon Blanc,
Steelhead Red (Rhône-
style blend), Syrah,
Zinfandel.

SPECIALTY: Limited-
production, single-
vineyard Zinfandels.

WINEMAKER: Grady Wann.

ANNUAL PRODUCTION:
23,000 cases.

OF SPECIAL NOTE: Patio
for picnickers. Annual
events include Hog
Island Oyster Weekend
(February), Grape
Stomping Contest
(October), and Library
Release weekend
(Thanksgiving). Petite
Sirah and Mourvèdre Rosé
available only at winery.

NEARBY ATTRACTIONS:
Lake Sonoma (boating,
camping, hiking).

First things first: The name is pronounced "kee-VEER-ah." Not only is the word intriguing, but it also connotes the winery owners' other passion: collecting antique maps. Henry and Holly Wendt, who have been acquiring these rare and beautiful documents since 1962, decided to name their winery after the legendary kingdom of Quivira, shown on many of their sixteenth- and seventeenth-century maps in the area now known as Sonoma County. The Wendts have loaned their extensive collection for a traveling exhibit. Following the tour, the maps will reside permanently at the winery.

In the early 1980s, the Wendts purchased a ninety-acre parcel with well-established vineyards in the Dry Creek Valley of Northern California. They developed Quivira in stages, focusing on a hillside vineyard that was planted to Zinfandel in the 1960s, planting more grape varieties, and making their own wine at neighboring wineries. From the beginning, they were aware of the appellation's fragile environment and practiced a minimalist form of agriculture to avoid interfering with natural cycles. They also chose grape varieties that were known to thrive in the

valley's particular soil and climatic conditions. With the assistance of a professional winemaker, the Wendts produced their first wines from the 1983 harvest: three hundred cases of Sauvignon Blanc and Zinfandel. Today they are proud that the vineyard is fully organic and biodynamic.

In 1987, the Wendts built their own winery. Set amid Zinfandel and Petite Sirah vineyards, the steep-roofed, earth-toned winery is reminiscent of the Sonoma County barns that inspired its design. The beautifully landscaped courtyard surrounding the winery, filled with roses, lavender, and olive trees, invites picnickers to drink in the dramatic vineyard and valley views, making this spot an idyllic site for the winery's frequent weekend events.

Winemaker Grady Wann joined Quivira in 1990 and has been making highly acclaimed, award-winning artisan wines since. He has assisted the Wendts in another pursuit: restoring the creek that bisects the property in order to bring back the steelhead trout once so populous here. The Wendts built low-fall dams that both collect gravel to create the perfect spawning beds for steelhead and form deep cool pools for the fish to rest on their long journey upstream. The Wendts also planted grasses, trees, and other vegetation along the banks. Each year the steelhead population returns in larger numbers, and in springtime visitors can spot them in the shallow waters.

RAVENSWOOD WINERY

Few wineries set out to make cult wines, and probably fewer to produce more than 400,000 cases a year. Ravenswood has done both. Its founders began by crushing enough juice to make 327 cases of Zinfandel in 1976, and although the winery also makes other wines, Zinfandel remains king. Nearly three-quarters of Ravenswood's production is Zinfandel.

Winemaker and cofounder Joel Peterson and chairman and cofounder Reed Foster were so successful with that first, handcrafted vintage that they have had to live up to the standard it set ever since. Ravenswood produces fourteen different Zinfandels that represent the spectrum of the varietal's personality, with tastes ranging from  peppery and spicy to chocolaty and minty. If there is one common denominator, it is reflected in the slogan adopted by the winery in 1990: "No Wimpy Wines."

Most of Ravenswood's grapes come from more than a hundred independent growers. It is those long-standing relationships that ensure the consistency of the wines. One vineyard source dates to 1986. The Strotz family invited Joel Peterson to visit their Sonoma Mountain vineyard, which they had named Pickberry because of all the wild blackberries harvested there. Peterson immediately recognized the quality of the Strotz grapes, and in 1988, Ravenswood released the first of its many blends of Cabernet Sauvignon, Cabernet Franc, and Merlot under the vineyard-designated name Pickberry.

Peterson never set out to specialize in Zinfandel; originally he was more interested in the Bordeaux varietals he began tasting at the age of ten with his father, Walter, founder of the San Francisco Wine Sampling Club. In time, however, he fell under the spell of Zinfandel. In the 1970s, after a brief career as a wine writer and consultant, he went to work for the late Joseph Swan, considered one of California's outstanding craftsmen of fine Zinfandel. Thus the stage was set for the varietal's ascendancy at the winery Peterson founded.

Ravenswood farms fourteen acres of estate vineyards on the northeast side of Sonoma. The old stone building, once home to the Haywood Winery, has extensive patio seating with beautiful south-facing views of the vineyards. Thanks to the company's growth, the winemaking operations have since been relocated to a forty-five-thousand-square-foot facility in the Carneros District, but the tasting room remains. Originally a cozy, even cramped affair, it was greatly expanded in 1996, and now has plenty of elbow room as well as ample natural light to sample and appreciate the wines.

RAVENSWOOD WINERY
18701 Gehricke Rd.
Sonoma, CA 95476
707-938-1960
888-669-4679
rwwine@ravenswood-wine.com
www.ravenswood-wine.com

OWNER: Franciscan Estates, Fine Wine Division of Constellation Brands.

LOCATION: About .5 mile northeast of town of Sonoma via Fourth St. East and Lovall Valley Rd.

APPELLATION: Sonoma Valley.

HOURS: 10 A.M.–4:30 P.M. daily.

TASTINGS: $5 for 5 wines; $10 for reserve wines.

TOURS: 10:30 A.M. daily, by appointment.

THE WINES: Bordeaux-style blends, Cabernet Franc, Cabernet Sauvignon, Chardonnay, ICON (Rhone-style blend), Merlot, Petite Sirah, Zinfandel.

SPECIALTY: Zinfandel.

WINEMAKER: Joel Peterson.

ANNUAL PRODUCTION: 400,000 cases.

OF SPECIAL NOTE: Bicyclists and other visitors are welcome to picnic on stone patio with view of vineyards.

NEARBY ATTRACTIONS: Mission San Francisco Solano and other historic buildings in downtown Sonoma; bike rentals; Vella Cheese Company; Sonoma Cheese Factory; Train Town (rides for children).

RAYMOND BURR VINEYARDS

RAYMOND BURR VINEYARDS
8339 West Dry Creek Rd.
Healdsburg, CA 95448
707-433-8559
Rbwyn@aol.com
www.raymondburrvineyards.com

OWNER: Robert Benevides.

LOCATION: 8.5 miles west of Healdsburg via Dry Creek Rd. and Yoakim Bridge Rd.

APPELLATION: Dry Creek Valley.

HOURS: 11 A.M.–5 P.M. daily.

TASTINGS: Complimentary.

TOURS: None of winery.

THE WINES: Cabernet Franc, Cabernet Sauvignon, Chardonnay.

SPECIALTY: Hillside Vineyard Cabernet Sauvignon.

WINEMAKER: John Quinones.

ANNUAL PRODUCTION: 3,000 cases.

OF SPECIAL NOTE: Orchid greenhouse tours Saturdays and Sundays by appointment with minimum of 8 guests; picnic area with view of Dry Creek Valley; monthly food-and-wine tastings.

NEARBY ATTRACTIONS: Lake Sonoma (boating, camping, hiking).

In 1986, some thirty years after the hit television show *Perry Mason* made Raymond Burr a household name, the actor decided to follow another passion: making great wine. The small Dry Creek Valley estate that bears his name does not produce enough grapes to find the worldwide audience of a hit TV series, but its reputation is growing.

Burr met fellow actor Robert Benevides on the set of *Perry Mason,* and they soon discovered that they shared an interest in appreciating wine and growing orchids. Eventually, the two friends turned both hobbies into viable commercial operations. In 1976, Benevides purchased forty prime acres of benchland at the foot of Bradford Mountain west of Healdsburg. As Burr's series *Ironside* was ending its eight-year run, the actor got his first look at the ranch. He must have been pleased: the view from the east-facing slopes of the property takes in a scenic swath of countryside, with hills and manzanita trees as far as the eye can see. In 1980, they relocated the commercial orchid nursery established several years earlier to the ranch and began developing the property.

The intimate, bungalow-style tasting room is filled with memorabilia from Raymond Burr's acting career, notably his Emmy awards and vintage issues of *TV Guide* with his picture on the covers. The space is cozy, so unless the weather is dismal, visitors take their glasses out to the patio, where they can be served in the shade of an old oak tree and take in the sweeping views. Sensational orchids can be seen in the greenhouses year-round, but fall is peak bloom season.

The fourteen-acre vineyard is on a steeply terraced hillside with very well-drained soil, ideal conditions for premium Cabernet Sauvignon grapes. Although the Dry Creek Valley is a warm growing region, the east-facing vineyards are bathed in shade late in the day, and the cool air from the nearby ocean keeps the temperatures low at night. The combination allows the grapes to mature at a steady pace. The longer the fruit hangs on the vine, the more flavor it develops. As John Quinones, who joined Raymond Burr Vineyards as winemaker in 1998, says, "A winemaker can't create quality. It's our job to preserve and enhance what comes out of the vineyard." Currently the vineyard includes nine acres of Cabernet Sauvignon, five acres of Chardonnay, and two acres of Cabernet Franc. Sadly, Burr's health deteriorated as the vineyards thrived, and he passed away in 1993. But a comment he made in a documentary about Northern California wines reflected his thinking about the vital, even intimate relationship between grape grower and land: "The most important things in a vineyard are the footprints of the grower between the rows."

SCHUG CARNEROS ESTATE WINERY

Fog and wind from the Pacific Ocean and San Francisco Bay sweep along the low, rocky hills of the Carneros appellation, where the volcanic soil, laden with clay, is shallow and dense. Grape growers intent on producing Cabernet Sauvignon and many other premium varietals avoid these conditions at all costs. But Walter Schug wanted to grow Pinot Noir, and he knew that this challenging combination of climate and geology would bring out the best in his favorite grape.

Schug first made his reputation in the 1970s as the acclaimed winemaker for Joseph Phelps. Working at the ultrapremium Napa Valley winery, he was successful with a range of wine grapes, notably Cabernet Sauvignon, before turning his attention to Pinot Noir. In 1980, beginning with grapes from a vineyard he had used at Phelps, Schug launched his own brand.

Schug and his wife, Gertrud, selected a fifty-acre site in the southern Sonoma Valley for their new vineyard estate and crowned the hilltop with a winery in 1990. They favored post-and-beam architecture reminiscent of  Germany's Rhine River Valley, where the Schug family had long produced Pinot Noir. The style makes it one of the most instantly recognizable wineries in the appellation. Pinot Noir and Chardonnay vineyards surround the winery, and Schug has long-term contracts with other growers in the Carneros to ensure the best grapes year after year. Protecting and enhancing the varietal and regional characteristics of the fruit are the essence of the Schug family's philosophy.

The European aspect of the Schug estate was enhanced with the excavation of an underground cave system in the mid-1990s. The system's naturally stable temperatures and humidity levels allow the wines to age gracefully in French oak barrels. Almost every inch of the caves is covered with gray concrete, but an exposed patch at the end of one tunnel affords a glimpse of the pockmarked, pumicelike volcanic rock characteristic of the region.

Visitors are warmly welcomed at this family-managed winery. From the hilltop tasting room, they are treated to spectacular views of the surrounding countryside and the northern reaches of San Francisco Bay. Nearby is a *pétanque* court, another nod to the Schugs' European ancestry. Newcomers and old hands alike are encouraged to play this French game, which requires dexterity in tossing a small ball to exactly the right spot. More than merely a sport, *pétanque* is a pastime that invites conviviality and conversation in the best old-world tradition.

SCHUG CARNEROS ESTATE WINERY
602 Bonneau Rd.
Sonoma, CA 95476
707-939-9363
800-966-9365
schug@schugwinery.com
www.schugwinery.com

OWNERS: Walter and Gertrud Schug.

LOCATION: .5 mile west of intersection of Hwy. 121 and Hwy. 116.

APPELLATION: Carneros.

HOURS: 10 A.M.–5 P.M. daily.

TASTINGS: Complimentary; $5 for reserve wines

TOURS: By appointment.

THE WINES: Cabernet Sauvignon, Chardonnay, Merlot, Pinot Noir, Sauvignon Blanc, Sparkling Pinot Noir.

SPECIALTY: Pinot Noir.

WINEMAKER: Michael Cox.

ANNUAL PRODUCTION: More than 20,000 cases.

OF SPECIAL NOTE: Open house in late April and in mid-November (Holiday in Carneros). *Pétanque* court open to public.

NEARBY ATTRACTIONS: Mission San Francisco Solano and other historic buildings in downtown Sonoma; Vintage Aircraft (scenic and aerobatic biplane rides); Infineon Raceway (auto racing); Viansa Winery Wetlands (tours).

SEGHESIO FAMILY VINEYARDS

SEGHESIO FAMILY VINEYARDS
14730 Grove St.
Healdsburg, CA 95448
707-433-7764
seghesio@seghesio.com
www.seghesio.com

OWNERS: Seghesio family.

LOCATION: About .5 mile southeast of Hwy. 101 via Dry Creek Rd. exit.

APPELLATION: Dry Creek Valley.

HOURS: 10 A.M.–5 P.M. daily.

TASTINGS: Complimentary.

TOURS: Self-guided tours through demonstration vineyards.

THE WINES: Arneis (white varietal from the Piedmont), Barbera, Cabernet Sauvignon/Sangiovese blend, Pinot Grigio, Pinot Noir, Sangiovese, Zinfandel.

SPECIALTY: Zinfandel.

WINEMAKER: Ted Seghesio.

ANNUAL PRODUCTION: 70,000 cases.

OF SPECIAL NOTE: Bocce ball courts. Shaded picnic tables.

NEARBY ATTRACTIONS: Lake Sonoma (boating, camping, hiking).

One of Sonoma's oldest and best-known families, the Seghesios have been growing grapes in the county since the nineteenth century. The cellar below the tasting room, for instance, dates to 1895 and has been restored on the footprint of the original winery. The tasting bar, ceiling, and doors are all fashioned from redwood milled from old wine tanks. Although parts of the structure are historic, the tasting room was built in 1997.

The saga of this winery began in 1895, when Italian immigrants Edoardo and Angela Seghesio, who had met while working at the Italian Swiss Colony winery, purchased a home and a fifty-six-acre ranch in Alexander Valley. Like other pioneering Italian families, the newlyweds brought centuries of agricultural and winemaking traditions to the New World. Their first vineyard was in a Sonoma County settlement called Chianti, where the railroad station was already bustling with business born of the region's emerging wine industry. By 1910, Edoardo had expanded his holdings by buying up the land around the station. Figuring that disembarking passengers would expect to find Chianti grapes in Chianti, he planted his "Chianti Station" vineyard largely to Sangiovese. Today, it is the oldest planting of Sangiovese in the United States. Four generations later, the Seghesios are still matching vineyards closely with the most appropriate varietals for each site. The family owns four hundred acres of vineyards in the Alexander, Dry Creek, and Russian River valleys. More than half are planted to Zinfandel.

The story of the Seghesio winery parallels the evolution of the Northern California wine industry from the earliest grapevines to today's premium wines. Edoardo continued to work at Italian Swiss Colony while constructing his own winery, which opened in 1902. In the years surrounding Prohibition, the vineyards and winery produced wine and sold it to local consumers by the gallon and to larger customers via railroad shipments. Following World War II, the family produced wine mainly for other wineries. It was not until 1983, at the encouragement of the younger generation, that the Seghesios began bottling wines under their own label. In 1995, a century after Edoardo bought his first vineyard, his descendants upgraded their vineyards and winery, decreased production, and increased the quality of their estate wines. Today, eight family members, representing the third, fourth, and fifth generations, are involved in the daily operations of the business.

ST. FRANCIS WINERY & VINEYARDS

Sonoma Valley's history as the site of the last and northernmost of the Spanish missions established in California is reflected in the stunning architecture of the St. Francis Winery. The red tile–roofed, sand-colored stucco building, faithful to early mission style, has a two-story tower with a bell that is rung to mark every hour. A statue of St. Francis welcomes visitors to the tasting room, where they are offered patio seating with breathtaking mountain and vineyard views. The visitor center opened in the spring of 2001, one mile west of the winery's former facility, completing the relocation of the entire operation. The new winery crowned thirty years of achievement by founder Joe Martin.

In 1971, the San Francisco businessman found himself in search of a change. He purchased the 1906 Behler Ranch in Kenwood and its hundred-acre vineyard, and began planting grapes that he sold to nearby wineries. Then, the following year, Martin was joined by his good friend, finance expert Lloyd Canton. Like many growers, the two eventually decided to build their own winery. St. Francis Winery, opened in 1979, is named after Saint Francis of Assisi, partly as a reference to the saint's role as a protector of animals and partly as an acknowledgment of the saint as a founder of the Franciscan order, which is credited with introducing European grape cultivation to the New World.

It is fitting that the one and only winemaker ever employed by St. Francis Winery & Vineyards was born and raised in San Francisco, a city also christened after the saint. Tom Mackey's arrival in 1983 ushered in a new direction at the winery: a heightened focus on red wines. When Mackey came on board, Martin and Canton added Cabernet Sauvignon and Zinfandel to the original mix of Chardonnay and Merlot. Over the next twenty years, St. Francis nurtured long-standing relationships with more than forty-five Sonoma County grape growers, which provided access to the Pagani Ranch and other enviable sources of old-vine Zinfandel grapes. Meanwhile, the winery developed more than five hundred acres of its own prime vineyards.

Among the wines previously produced from this diversity were Riesling, Gewürztraminer, Muscat, and Chardonnay, in addition to Merlot and Cabernet. Mackey gradually decreased the output of white wines from 80 percent when he arrived to 30 percent today, most of which is Chardonnay made from 100 percent Sonoma County grapes. With this change of focus to big, rich Cabernet, Merlot, and Zinfandel wines, St. Francis soon became known as "The House of Big Reds." Mackey has also created a series of small-lot single vineyard–designated wines available only at the visitor center.

ST. FRANCIS WINERY & VINEYARDS
100 Pythian Rd.
Santa Rosa, CA 95409
707-833-4666
800-543-7713
info@stfranciswine.com
www.stfranciswine.com

FOUNDING OWNER: Joseph Martin.

LOCATION: Off Hwy. 12, 6 miles east of Santa Rosa and 1 mile west of Kenwood.

APPELLATION: Sonoma Valley.

HOURS: 10 A.M.–5 P.M. daily.

TASTINGS: $5 for 4 wines.

TOURS: None.

THE WINES: Cabernet Sauvignon, Chardonnay, Merlot, Zinfandel.

SPECIALTIES: Reserve vineyard-designated Cabernet Sauvignon, Chardonnay, Merlot, Zinfandel.

WINEMAKER: Tom Mackey.

ANNUAL PRODUCTION: 250,000 cases.

OF SPECIAL NOTE: Single-vineyard wines sold only at winery. Annual events such as Barrel Tasting (March), Harvest in the Vineyards (September), Holiday Open House (November), and Festival of Lights (December). Elegant wine accessories at winery shop.

NEARBY ATTRACTIONS: Sugarloaf Ridge State Park (hiking, camping, horseback riding); Annadel State Park (hiking, biking).

VALLEY OF THE MOON WINERY

VALLEY OF THE MOON WINERY
777 Madrone Rd.
Glen Ellen, CA 95442
707-996-6941
luna@vomwinery.com
www.valleyofthemoon
winery.com

OWNER: Gary Heck.

LOCATION: 5 miles north of
the town of Sonoma via
Hwy. 12.

APPELLATION:
Sonoma Valley.

HOURS: 10 A.M.–4:30 P.M.
daily.

TASTINGS: Complimentary
for 4 wines; $2 for reserve
wines (applicable to
purchase).

TOURS: 10:30 A.M. and
2 P.M. daily.

THE WINES: Barbera,
Cabernet Sauvignon,
Chardonnay, Cuvée,
De La Luna (proprietary
red blend), old-vine
Zinfandel, Pinot Blanc,
Pinot Noir, Port, Rosata
Di Sangiovese, Sangiovese,
Sparkling Wine, Syrah,
Zinfandel.

SPECIALTIES: Cuvée De
La Luna, Pinot Blanc,
and Port.

WINEMAKER: Steve Rued.

ANNUAL PRODUCTION:
40,000 cases.

OF SPECIAL NOTE: Barbera,
Port, and sparkling wine
available only at winery.
Annual events include
Barrel Tasting (March),
Festa Italia (July), and
Harvest Moon (October).

NEARBY ATTRACTIONS:
Jack London Historic State
Park (museum, hiking,
horseback riding);
Sonoma Valley Regional
Park (hiking, dog park);
Mission San Francisco
Solano and other historic
buildings in downtown
Sonoma.

I f there's one undertaking more difficult than building a winery from scratch, it is transforming a historic winery into a facility capable of turning out first-rate wines. In 1997, that was the challenge facing the new owners of a winery established in 1863. Gary Heck, who also owns Korbel Champagne Cellars and Kenwood Vineyards, was determined to maintain the character of the original buildings. The decision to honor the winery's heritage found expression in an extensive renovation that kept the original stone walls of the winery and fermentation building and preserved the estate's old-vine Zinfandel vineyards and its landmark 400-year-old bay tree.

Heck decided to build a new winemaking facility next to the original fermentation room, which was designated for a new tasting room. The first task was to uncover the twenty-seven-ton, twenty-inch-thick stone walls built  in 1863 by Chinese stone masons who stayed on in the Sonoma Valley after their work on the railroads was completed. Preserving the winery's unreinforced walls, buried beneath decades of piecemeal additions, was particularly delicate work since they had to be braced to withstand earthquakes. When it came to the exterior of the new winery facility, the architect showed respect for the agricultural setting by using materials such as board and batten with metal roofs. For the color palette, the designers had to look no further than the old vines that turn red and gold in autumn. The exterior of the tasting room was plastered with a three-color, hand-troweled finish. Zinclike metal roofs, sliding barn doors, open trusses, and other early California construction details unite the new building complex.

The winery land was once part of the 48,000-acre Agua Caliente Land Grant owned by General Mariano Vallejo. In 1863 the "Stone Tract" portion was conveyed to George Whitman, the first owner to grow grapes and build a winery. Years later, the property was purchased by Senator George Hearst, father of newspaper magnate William Randolph Hearst. Senator Hearst further developed Madrone Vineyards, as it was then called, into a serious winemaking operation.

Visitors today taste wines in an 1,800-square-foot room that a century ago was filled with concrete fermentation tanks. Given rich texture with stone, metal, and hand-colored concrete, the tasting room has oversized casement windows that open out to the old-vine Zinfandel vineyard. A graceful, curvilinear wine bar is sheathed in a metal quilt of bronze, copper, and stainless steel—the same dimpled stainless steel used for the winery's steel fermentation tanks. Visible behind the tasting bar is one of the original stone walls.

VIANSA WINERY & ITALIAN MARKETPLACE

Looking like a village in the Italian countryside, the terra-cotta villa and its grove of olive trees crown a knoll in the southern Sonoma Valley. If the spot reminds travelers of Tuscany, it's no surprise: Viansa proprietor Sam Sebastiani traces his ancestry to the region.

A member of the third generation of Sebastianis to make wine in Sonoma, Sam served as president of Sebastiani Vineyards from 1980 to 1986 and is generally credited with shifting the winery's emphasis from bulk wine to premium varietals. When he and his wife, Vicki, decided to establish their own winery, they saw an opportunity to distinguish themselves by focusing on Italian varietals and giving food equal billing. They chose to call their place Viansa, a combination of their first names. Sam's winemaking talents, Vicki's culinary expertise, and hundred-plus acres of estate vineyards proved to be a winning combination. Three of their seven children work at the winery: Jon is president, Lisa is public relations manager, and Joe is vineyard, olive grove, and wetlands manager.

Viansa Winery, opened in 1990, produces the largest selection of Italian varietals of any American winery. In the early days, Viansa was known mostly for Chardonnay and Cabernet Sauvignon but has gradually increased its production of Italian wines from five thousand to fifty thousand cases a year.

The two tasting bars in the Italian Marketplace pour samples of Italian varietals that have gained recognition in the United States, such as Sangiovese and Pinot Grigio, as well as less-familiar ones like Nebbiolo, Barbera, and Arneis. The marketplace is a mecca for food lovers who know they can find dozens of condiments, marinades, and sauces, samples of which are offered for impromptu tastings. For heartier fare, the *cucina* (Italian kitchen) prepares fresh salads, sandwiches, tortas, and desserts that can be taken out to one of the shaded picnic tables. From this perch, picnickers can enjoy the north-facing view of the Sonoma Valley, wedged between the Mayacamas Range to the east and the forested slopes of Sonoma Mountain to the west.

Directly north of the winery are ninety acres of lowlands that are flooded on a seasonal basis, rendering the site useless for grape growing. In 1992, Sam Sebastiani, a longtime conservationist and outdoorsman, began establishing a wetlands preserve that supports a variety of wildlife, including owls, egrets, tundra swans, golden eagles, Canada geese, and several species of ducks. More than 150 avian species have been spotted here, with more than 13,000 birds visiting each day during peak migratory periods in late winter and early spring. Sebastiani relishes knowing that he has provided valuable habitat by creating the county's largest privately owned, freshwater wetlands.

VIANSA WINERY & ITALIAN MARKETPLACE
25200 Arnold Dr.
Sonoma, CA 95476
707-935-4700
800-995-4740
tuscan@viansa.com
www.viansa.com

FOUNDERS: Sam and Vicki Sebastiani.

LOCATION: About 5 miles south of the town of Sonoma.

APPELLATION: Carneros.

HOURS: 10 A.M.–5 P.M. daily.

TASTINGS: Complimentary for 4 wines; $5 for 3 reserve wines.

TOURS: Guided tours of winery ($5) 11 A.M. and 2 P.M. daily; self-guided tours during operating hours. Two-hour wetlands tours ($15) on alternate Sundays, February–May.

THE WINES: Aleatico, Arneis, Barbera, Cabernet Franc, Cabernet Sauvignon, Chardonnay, Dolcetto, Freisa, Merlot, Moscata Grappa, Muscat Canelli, Nebbiolo, Pinot Grigio, Primitivo, Sangiovese, Sauvignon Blanc, Teroldego, Tocai Friulano, Vernaccia, Zinfandel.

SPECIALTIES: Italian varietals.

WINEMAKER: Derek Irwin.

ANNUAL PRODUCTION: 56,000 cases.

OF SPECIAL NOTE: Italian deli; outdoor barbecue on select weekends in spring and summer. Food and tabletop accessories at marketplace.

NEARBY ATTRACTIONS: Mission San Francisco Solano and other historic buildings in downtown Sonoma; Infineon Raceway (auto racing); Vintage Aircraft (scenic and aerobatic biplane rides).

MENDOCINO

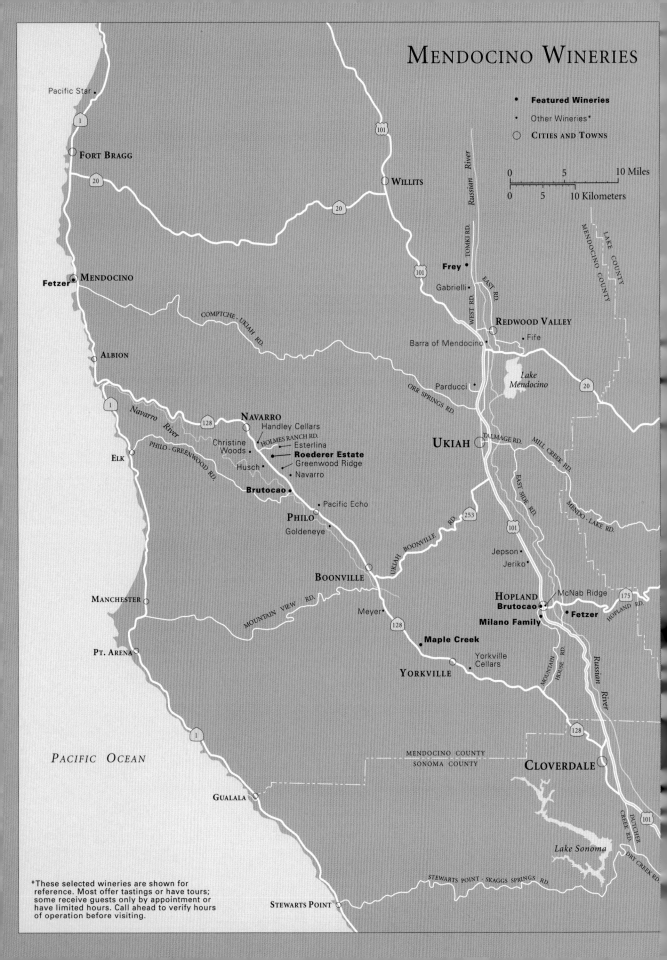

Mendocino Wineries

Featured Wineries
Other Wineries*
Cities and Towns

*These selected wineries are shown for reference. Most offer tastings or have tours; some receive guests only by appointment or have limited hours. Call ahead to verify hours of operation before visiting.

Inland Mendocino has been slower to catch national attention than the county's dramatic coastline has, but that is changing as local winemakers prove that their grapes are on a par with those of Sonoma and Napa. There remains something of a pioneer spirit here, a love of the great outdoors that is reflected in a serious respect for the environment. It is no wonder that Mendocino leads the nation in farming organic vineyards.

Many Mendocino wineries are located off the beaten path in the shelter of redwoods or beside rivers. Most of the county is undeveloped, a pristine landscape with abundant opportunities for hiking, fishing, camping, and other outdoor pursuits.

Wine grapes were first planted here in the middle of the nineteenth century, some by immigrants drawn to California by the 1849 Gold Rush. These farmers tended to plant food crops on the flat river plains and to position their vineyards on the more rugged hillsides and sun-exposed ridgetops. In time, they and their successors found fertile ground in the cooler Anderson Valley west of Hopland and Ukiah. The growing conditions vary so greatly between these two regions that Mendocino winemakers have found success with a wide spectrum of grape varietals.

BRUTOCAO CELLARS

Downtown Hopland was a quiet place with only a hotel, two modest restaurants, a brew pub, and the odd antique shop until the Brutocao family came to town. The Brutocaos, who had been making wine under their own label and already operated a tasting room in nearby Anderson Valley, decided to establish a presence on U.S. 101.

In 1997, Brutocao Cellars purchased the old Hopland High School from the Fetzer wine family and began creating a seven-and-a-half-acre complex dedicated to food and wine. Schoolhouse Plaza opened two years later with a tasting room, a gift shop, and the Crushed Grape Restaurant in the remodeled 1920s building, which still has its original facade bearing the high school's name. On display in the tasting room and restaurant are memorabilia from the school's glory days. The complex also includes a coffee shop, an art gallery, and a store featuring locally made products. Visitors can sip coffee while perusing the racks in the adjacent visitors' center.

The Brutocaos, who trace their heritage to Italy, brought more than a love of food and wine when they came to this country. They are also passionate about bocce ball, a devilishly challenging game with a half-century Italian lineage. The complex has six regulation bocce (pronounced BOTCH-ee) courts, which are lighted and open to the public.

With the remodeling complete, the winery set to work landscaping the grounds with some six thousand lavender plants and thirty-four hundred rosebushes. Between the terraces and the bocce ball courts is an expanse of manicured lawn with a peaked-roof gazebo that is used for weddings and other special events.

Brutocao Cellars is a tale of two families who combined their skills and expertise to establish one of Mendocino County's most notable wineries. The Brutocaos immigrated from Venice in the early 1900s, bringing with them a passion for wine. Len Brutocao met Marty Bliss while in school at Berkeley. Marty's father, Irv, had been farming land in Mendocino since the 1940s. Len and Marty married, and soon thereafter the families joined forces and began to grow grapes. The family sold their grapes to other wineries for years before starting to make their own wine in 1991. They selected the Lion of St. Mark from St. Mark's Cathedral in Venice as their symbol of family tradition and quality. The heart of that quality, they say, is in their 575 acres of vineyards in southern Mendocino County and another 12 acres (of Pinot Noir) in Anderson Valley. The original tasting room in Philo is still in use. With its high-beamed ceilings and wisteria-covered patio, it makes an ideal stop for those traveling scenic Highway 128 to the Pacific Coast.

BRUTOCAO CELLARS
13500 Hwy. 101
Hopland, CA 95449
800-433-3689
7000 Hwy. 128
Philo, CA 95466
707-895-2152
brutocao@pacific.net
www.brutocaocellars.com

OWNER: Leonard Brutocao.

LOCATION: U.S. 101 in downtown Hopland; Hwy. 128 in Anderson Valley.

APPELLATION: Mendocino.

HOURS: 10 A.M.–5 P.M. daily.

TASTINGS: Complimentary.

TOURS: By appointment.

THE WINES: Cabernet Sauvignon, Chardonnay, Merlot, Pinot Noir, Port, Primitivo, Sauvignon Blanc, Syrah, Zinfandel.

SPECIALTIES: Cabernet Sauvignon, Merlot, Zinfandel.

WINEMAKER: Fred Nickel.

ANNUAL PRODUCTION: 12,000 cases.

OF SPECIAL NOTE: Port and Syrah available only at tasting rooms. Crushed Grape Restaurant serving wood-fired pizza and California cuisine. Annual events include Valentine's Day Crabfeed (February), Cioppino Feed Bocce Tourney (April), Hopland Passport (May and October), Anderson Valley Pinot Noir Festival (May), Big Bottles and Bocce BBQ (June), Port and Chocolate Tasting (November).

NEARBY ATTRACTIONS: Real Goods Solar Living Center (tours, store); Fetzer Organic Gardens (tours); Hendy Woods State Park (redwood groves, hiking, camping).

FETZER VINEYARDS

FETZER VINEYARDS
13601 Old River Rd.
Hopland, CA 95449
707-744-1250
45070 Main St.
Mendocino, CA 95460
800-860-3347
800-846-8637
www.fetzer.com

OWNER: Brown-Forman
Corporation.

LOCATIONS: 1 mile east of
U.S. 101 in Hopland via
Hwy. 175; Mendocino
Village, next to Mendocino
Hotel.

APPELLATION: Mendocino.

HOURS: 9 A.M.–5 P.M. daily.

TASTINGS: Complimentary
tastings of Fetzer and
Bonterra organically
grown wines.

TOURS: Tours of garden
three times daily May–
September.

THE WINES: Cabernet
Sauvignon, Chardonnay,
Gewürztraminer,
Johannisberg Riesling,
Merlot, Pinot Noir,
Sauvignon Blanc, Syrah,
White Zinfandel, Zinfandel.

SPECIALTIES: Reserve
Collection, Five Rivers
Ranch wines.

WINEMAKER: Dennis Martin.

ANNUAL PRODUCTION:
4 million cases.

OF SPECIAL NOTE: 10-room
inn. Special garden and
culinary events and
demonstrations throughout
year. Heirloom seeds, oils
and vinegars flavored with
organic herbs from Fetzer's
garden, and gourmet foods
sold at winery. Picnic tables
provided.

NEARBY ATTRACTIONS:
Real Goods Solar Living
Center (tours, store); Vichy
Springs (mineral springs
and resort).

In essence, growing grapes is an agricultural endeavor, requiring the same kind of expertise, perseverance, and responsible farming practices as any other crop. Nowhere is the link between successful grape growing and respect for the environment more evident than at the Fetzer Vineyards Valley Oaks Ranch in scenic southern Mendocino County.

The Fetzer family has spent more than twenty years improving the winery's energy efficiency and vineyard practices, and the sustainability of its general business operations. In addition to composting and recycling, Fetzer is the only winery in the United States to have its oak barrels built on-site and to operate an in-house oak-barrel restoration program that adds years to the life of a wine barrel. Most importantly, Fetzer has become an industry leader in farming grapes organically. It also has encouraged other growers to adopt similar practices and has supported them in their efforts by sharing information and expertise.

At the same time, Fetzer pursues a winemaker's ultimate goal: the production of high-quality wines that are popular and critical successes. The winery's premium varietals, Five Rivers Ranch and Barrel Select wines, and Reserve Collection have won top awards at national and international competitions.

The wines are only one of many reasons to visit the ninety-five-acre Valley Oaks Ranch. While many wineries support the idea of linking wine with food, Fetzer has taken the concept to its logical extension by planting an extensive organic garden of fruits, vegetables, and herbs, along with flowers. Within the five acres, visitors find a number of special gardens with clearly labeled plants. In the Mediterranean Walk, a canopy of pomegranates, figs, and olives shelters aromatic herbs and other plants. A gazebo and a fountain provide focal points in the Reserve Garden of roses and wisteria. In the Border of Life are flowers that attract hummingbirds and butterflies as well as beneficial insects. Strolling through these lush and prolific gardens—either independently or with Garden Director Kate Frey—gives visitors vivid and memorable impressions of the sustainable growing practices in use throughout the Fetzer properties. It's also permissible to carry a glass of wine along for some on-the-spot pairings with fruits and vegetables. If that leaves visitors hungry, they can purchase sandwiches, salads, or pastas in the spacious Garden Café, which also houses the tasting room.

Along with special in-depth garden seminars and demonstrations, Fetzer offers cooking classes and food-and-wine events led by Culinary Director John Ash, an internationally recognized chef, educator, and author.

FETZER
VINEYARDS

TASTING ROOM

FREY VINEYARDS, LTD.

Arguably the most low-key winery in California, this gem is hidden off a two-lane road that wends through an undeveloped corner of Redwood Valley. Unsuspecting visitors might mistake the first building for the tasting room, but that's grandma's house. They must drive past it to reach the winery, and upon arriving, they find that there is no formal tasting room. Instead, tastings are conducted outdoors at a couple of planks set over a pair of wine barrels. When temperatures drop or rain falls, everyone retires to the original house—a redwood structure fashioned from an old barn—where the senior Mrs. Frey lives. Visitors are encouraged to picnic at one of several redwood tables and benches hand-hewn by the late family patriarch, Paul.

Virtually everything at this winery seems handmade or fashioned from something else. Barrels and tanks have been salvaged from larger operations, and the winery itself was constructed of redwood from a defunct winery in  Ukiah. Some rows of grapevines are interplanted with herbs such as sage and oregano, which are harvested and distilled into aromatherapy products.

Frey (pronounced "fry") Vineyards is the oldest and largest all-organic winery in the United States. It may have another claim to fame as the winery with the most family members on the payroll. In 1961, Paul and Marguerite Frey, both doctors, bought ninety-nine acres near the headwaters of the Russian River. The Redwood Valley property seemed a great place to raise a family. Five of the couple's twelve children were born after the move, and most are still in the neighborhood.

In 1965, the Freys planted forty acres of Cabernet Sauvignon and Grey Riesling grapevines on the ranch's old pastureland, but they didn't start making wine until the 1970s. Eldest son Jonathan, who studied organic viticulture, began tending the vineyards and harvesting the grapes, which at first were sold to other wineries. When a Cabernet Sauvignon made with their grapes won a gold medal for a Santa Cruz winery, the family realized the vineyard's potential. Frey Vineyards was founded the next year, in 1980.

In 1996, the family began farming biodynamically. The word *biodynamic* stems from the agricultural theories of Austrian scientist and educator Rudolf Steiner. Biodynamic practices undertake to restore vitality to the soil. The farm is managed as a self-sustaining ecosystem, using special composting methods and specific planting times. As good stewards of the land, Frey started the first organic winery and is now the first American winery fully certified by Demeter, the biodynamic certification organization. The wines have won many gold and silver medals for excellence.

FREY VINEYARDS, LTD.
14000 Tomki Rd.
Redwood Valley, CA 95470
707-485-5177
800-760-3739
info@freywine.com
www.freywine.com

OWNERS: Frey family.

LOCATION: 14 miles north of Ukiah off U.S. 101.

APPELLATION: Redwood Valley.

HOURS: By appointment.

TASTINGS: Complimentary.

TOURS: By appointment.

THE WINES: Cabernet Sauvignon, Chardonnay, Gewürztraminer, Merlot, Petite Sirah, Pinot Noir, Sangiovese, Sauvignon Blanc, Syrah, Zinfandel.

SPECIALTIES: Certified organic wines without added sulfites; biodynamically grown estate-bottled wines.

WINEMAKERS: Paul and Jonathan Frey.

ANNUAL PRODUCTION: 60,000 cases.

OF SPECIAL NOTE: Picnic area for visitors' use; biodynamic aromatherapy products made from vineyard-grown herbs sold at winery.

NEARBY ATTRACTIONS: Real Goods Solar Living Center (tours, store); Lake Mendocino (hiking, boating, fishing, camping); Grace Hudson Museum (Pomo Indian baskets, historical photographs, changing art exhibits); Vichy Springs (mineral springs and resort); Orr Hot Springs (mineral springs spa).

MAPLE CREEK WINERY

MAPLE CREEK WINERY
20799 Hwy. 128
Yorkville CA 95494
707-895-3001
Linda@maplecreekwine.com;
Tom@maplecreekwine.com
www.artevinowine.com
www.maplecreekwine.com

OWNERS: Tom Rodrigues
and Linda Stutz.

LOCATION: 22 miles west of
Cloverdale via Hwy. 128.

APPELLATION:
Yorkville Highlands.

HOURS: 10:30 A.M.–5 P.M.
daily; shorter hours in the
winter months.

TASTINGS: $3 (applicable
to purchase).

TOURS: None.

THE WINES: Chardonnay,
Merlot, Pinot Noir,
Symphony (hybrid of
Muscat and Grenache
Gris), Zinfandel.

SPECIALTIES: Estate
Chardonnay, late-harvest
wines, Bordeaux-style reds.

WINEMAKER:
Tom Rodrigues; Kerry
Damskey, consulting
winemaker.

ANNUAL PRODUCTION:
2,500 cases.

OF SPECIAL NOTE: Art
gallery featuring works by
owner/winemaker Tom
Rodrigues. Picnic tables.
Most of the wines available
only at the tasting room.
Local events include Crab
and Wine Days (January),
Yorkville Highlands Wine
Festival (June), and
Mushroom and Wine Days
(November).

NEARBY ATTRACTIONS:
Hendy Woods State Park
(redwood groves, hiking,
camping).

In late winter and early spring, drivers along scenic Highway 128 can see young lambs cavorting in the fields, a sure sign of impending warm weather. Throughout the year, apple and pear orchards, small farms, and winding roads make this part of Mendocino one of the most beautiful drives in California. It is characterized by small, family-owned wineries where the owners and winemakers are often available to meet visitors. Life at Maple Creek is so casual, in fact, that if you arrive in the winter months, you may be greeted by a sign that reads "Honk For Wine."

That potential for an intimate experience was one of the factors in Linda Stutz's and Tom Rodrigues's decision to open their own winery. The couple met at a party in 1995, when both were pursuing their own careers. Stutz  was designing commercial interiors in San Francisco. Rodrigues had established himself as a successful artist in media ranging from stained glass to wine labels, such as those for Far Niente and its sister winery, Nickel & Nickel, in Napa Valley.

By 2001, Stutz and Rodrigues were ready for a radical change. When the old Martz family property came on the market, they recognized a good business opportunity. The 180-acre parcel included seven natural springs and was far from the hectic urban environment of the San Francisco Bay Area. Today, they own 12 acres of vineyards and still have plenty of room for their menagerie of sheep, horses, dogs, and cats to roam.

Stutz and Rodrigues named their winery after the creek that runs year-round through their hilly property and set to work transforming a rundown farm building into a rustic tasting room. They decorated it with numerous paintings and other works by Rodrigues, ranging from a portrait of baseball player Cool Papa Bell (the original hangs in the Hall of Fame in Cooperstown, New York) to pastoral scenes of Anderson Valley, which adorn the winery's Artevino label. Rodrigues and Stutz chose the name to represent their twin interests.

Rodrigues was introduced to wine as a youngster. His grandparents earned their living growing fruit, and wine was regarded as merely one more food product on the dining room table. By the time he was an adult, Rodrigues had become a serious wine consumer and collector. He is still learning, thanks to his winemaking consultant, Kerry Damskey, who has done similar work for prestigious labels such as Flora Springs and Preston.

Rodrigues and Stutz, like a handful of colleagues in the sparsely populated Yorkville Highlands appellation, have become not only vintners but ranchers and art dealers as well. That their nearest neighbors are at least a mile away suits them just fine.

MILANO FAMILY WINERY

What looks like a big, old barnlike structure set back from the highway was built in 1947 not as a winery but as a hop kiln. The building is just south of downtown Hopland, which got its name from the period—late 1800s through mid-1900s—when the growing and processing of hops were important industries in Mendocino County. The dried cones of the hop flowers are a major ingredient in beer.

The hop business was still booming in the 1940s when Vincenzo Milone and his son, Frank, who had been farming pears, prunes, and grapes as well as hops on the surrounding acres, decided to replace a kiln burned down in the late 1930s by a moonshiner. In 1954, when the demand for local hops died out, the facility closed its doors. Twenty-two years later, Vincenzo's grandson, Jim, transformed the old kiln into a winery, the Milano Family Winery. The current owners, Deanna and Ted Starr, bought the winery in 2001. The couple had their own businesses in Southern California and were visiting acquaintances in nearby Sonoma when they heard of a winery for sale in an unfamiliar place called Hopland. They drove up to see it and fell in love with the old building, the town, and the rolling hills dotted with oak trees. They found it surprisingly easy to give up their hurried life for rustic Mendocino County.

The Starrs are happy to show visitors how hops were originally processed, along with the current winemaking activities. The structure is one of only three hop kilns remaining in the county and the only one open to the public. The entire tasting room, including the bar, is made of heart redwood. The tall tasting bar is the perfect height to rest your elbows on as you begin to unwind while sipping one of Milano's handmade wine selections.

The Starrs plan to keep production at about four thousand cases so special care can be given to every barrel. Ted, a software developer for the past several years, has created a program to manage tasting rooms, wine clubs, and inventory. Winemaker Deanna's background is in nursing and home health administration, but her hobby is gourmet cooking. As she notes, her nursing knowledge has helped her understand the chemistry of winemaking, and her cooking experience has taught her about balancing flavors.

Visitors to the winery often buy a bottle to enjoy at picnic tables set in the shade of a trellis, where they have views of the Sanel Valley. Sometimes they linger to visit with Buster the donkey in the horse pasture or Willie the potbellied pig and the pair of pygmy goats, Spic and Span, along with chickens, ducks, and curly-feathered geese.

MILANO FAMILY WINERY
14594 South Hwy. 101
Hopland, CA 95449
707-744-1396
wines@milanowinery.com
www.milanowinery.com

OWNERS: Ted and Deanna Starr.

LOCATION: About .5 mile south of Hopland.

APPELLATION: Mendocino.

HOURS: 10 A.M.–5 P.M. daily.

TASTINGS: Complimentary; $5 for reserve wines.

TOURS: By appointment.

THE WINES: Cabernet Sauvignon, Carignane, Chardonnay, Echo and Sanel (Bordeaux blends), Port, Sunshine (French Colombard/Muscat blend), Syrah, Zinfandel.

SPECIALTIES: Cabernet Sauvignon, Port, Zinfandel.

WINEMAKER: Deanna Starr.

ANNUAL PRODUCTION: 4,000 cases.

OF SPECIAL NOTE: Small percentage of wines distributed outside winery; bottle limits on library wines. Events include Hopland Passport (May and October) and frequent concerts at the winery.

NEARBY ATTRACTIONS: Fetzer Organic Gardens (tours); Vichy Springs (mineral springs and resort); Real Goods Solar Living Center (tours, store).

ROEDERER ESTATE

ROEDERER ESTATE
4501 Hwy. 128
Philo, CA 95466
707-895-2288
info@roedererestate.net
www.roedererestate.net

OWNERS: Champagne Louis
Roederer/Jean-Claude
Rouzaud.

LOCATION: About 6 miles
northwest of Philo.

APPELLATION:
Anderson Valley.

HOURS: 11 A.M.–5 P.M. daily.

TASTINGS:
$3 for 5 or 6 wines.

TOURS: By appointment.

THE WINES: Brut,
Brut Rosé, L'Ermitage,
Pinot Noir.

SPECIALTY: L'Ermitage.

WINEMAKER:
Arnaud Weyrich.

ANNUAL PRODUCTION:
90,000 cases.

OF SPECIAL NOTE: Pinot
Noir and jeroboams
(3-liter bottles) of Brut
and Brut Rosé sparkling
wines available only at
winery. Annual Anderson
Valley Pinot Noir Festival
(May).

NEARBY ATTRACTIONS:
Hendy Woods State
Park (redwood groves,
hiking, camping).

Roederer Estate is nestled in the cool, fog-shrouded Anderson Valley, where the climate and well-drained soils provide the ideal growing conditions for sparkling wine grapes. The estate's wines are made in the French style—by the *méthode champenoise*—an elaborate process whereby the wine is fermented for the second time in the actual bottle rather than in a tank. Although this type of fermentation takes longer, it produces a superior sparkling wine. Nothing less would be expected from this winery, whose parent company, Champagne Louis Roederer, has been in business in Reims, France, since 1776.

And as befits a winery in the southwest corner of Mendocino's Anderson Valley, the winery is made of redwood, instead of stone as is common in France. The facility, at forty-eight thousand square feet, does not look as large as it sounds. It is discreetly built into the hill, with large cellars set below ground level. The lawn is rimmed by a border of hardy perennials including agapanthus, daylilies, roses, yarrow, penstemon, and other varieties that provide lavender, yellow, pink, and red blossoms during much of the year.

The landscaping as well as the forested ridges to the west are clearly visible through large windows in the tasting room. An ornately carved ten-foot-tall antique armoire dominates the entrance. The other décor suggests the hand of someone French: there is plenty to amuse the eye but not so much that the space looks cluttered. An elegant tasting bar hand-carved of black walnut runs the length of one side of the room. On the opposite wall hangs a row of nine large prints of Emile Bourdelin wood carvings. The originals, commissioned by Louis Roederer, depict winery scenes from the early 1900s. Chairs and square tables are arrayed beneath the prints. At the far end of the room, a carefully selected collection of potted palms completes the effect of a Parisian bistro. Even the floor tiles are French. Red and as thick as bricks, they were made in the mid-eighteenth century and once graced a chateau in the old country.

Roederer Estate is a family-owned company whose owner, president Jean-Claude Rouzaud, is a fifth-generation descendant of the founder. He carefully selected the site of the winery, which comprises 480 acres of vineyards. About 60 percent of the acreage is planted in Chardonnay grapes, and the remainder, in Pinot Noir.

ACKNOWLEDGMENTS

Creativity, perseverance, and commitment all have important roles in guaranteeing the success
of a project. The artistic and editorial team who worked on this edition possesses these qualities
in large measures. My heartfelt thanks go to Marty Olmstead, writer; Robert Holmes, photographer;
Kari Ontko, designer; Judith Dunham, copyeditor, Carrie Bradley, proofreader;
Ben Pease, cartographer; and Kristen Wurz, layout production.

In addition, I am grateful for the invaluable counsel of Barbara Moulton, Greg Taylor,
my late-night crisis administrator, Danny Biederman, and the scores of readers and winery enthusiasts
who have contacted me to say how much they enjoyed the first edition.

And finally, for putting up with work-filled weekends and midnight deadlines, my gratitude
and enduring affection go to Gent and Lisa Silberkleit.

–Tom Silberkleit

Photographs copyright © 2004 by Robert Holmes
Text and maps copyright © 2004 by Wine House Press
All rights reserved. No text, photographs, maps, or other
portions of this book may be reproduced in any form
without the written permission of the publisher.

Wine House Press
127 East Napa Street, Suite F, Sonoma, CA 95476
707-996-1741

Editor and publisher: Tom Silberkleit
Original design: Jennifer Barry Design, Fairfax, CA
Design and production: Kari Ontko and Kristen Wurz
Copyeditor: Judith Dunham
Maps: Ben Pease
Proofreader: Carrie Bradley

All photographs by Robert Holmes except the following:
page 24, bottom left: Marvin Collins; page 28, bottom
left: Lenny Siegel Photographic; page 30: Kate Kline May;
page 31: John Sutton; page 32, bottom left: Rick Bolen;
page 39, bottom left: Adrian Gregorutti; page 46:
Frank Deras; page 47, bottom left: Jean DeLuca; page 51
bottom left: Rick Bolen; page 52, bottom right: Gundolf
Pfotenhauer; pages 72 and 73: creativedirections.com;
page 88, bottom left: Bill Dungan; page 91, bottom right:
Chris Vomvolakis; page104, bottom right: Chris
Vomvolakis; page 119, bottom right: Pradoe Advertising
and Design; pages 134 and 135: John Birchard;
page 140: Charles Starr.

Front cover photograph: Vineyards on Silverado Trail, Napa
Back cover photographs: top left: Spring Mountain
Vineyard; top right: Schug Carneros Estate Winery;
bottom left: Fritz Winery; bottom right: Mumm Napa.

Printed and bound in Singapore through DNP America,
LLC

ISBN 0-9724993-2-6

Second Edition

Distributed by Ten Speed Press, P.O. Box 7123, Berkeley, CA
94707, www.tenspeed.com

The publisher has made every effort to ensure the accuracy
of the information contained in *The California Directory of
Fine Wineries*, but can accept no liability for any loss, injury,
or inconvenience sustained by any visitor as a result of any
information or recommendation contained in this guide.
Travelers should always call ahead to confirm hours of
operation, fees, and other highly variable information.

Always act responsibly when drinking alcoholic beverages by
selecting a designated driver or prearranged transportation.

Customized Editions
Wine House Press will print custom editions of this volume
for bulk purchase at your request. Personalized covers and
foil-stamped corporate logo imprints can be created in large
quantities for special promotions or events, or as premiums.
For more information, contact Custom Imprints, Wine
House Press, 127 E. Napa Street, Suite F, Sonoma, CA 95476;
707-996-1741.